The Three Sisters

Homesteading Stories From Early Saskatchewan

HAZEL HARRIS

The Three Sisters
Copyright © 2022 by Hazel Harris

All rights reserved. No part of this publication may be reproduced, distributed, or transmitted in any form or by any means, including photocopying, recording, or other electronic or mechanical methods, without the prior written permission of the author, except in the case of brief quotations embodied in critical reviews and certain other non-commercial uses permitted by copyright law.

Special thanks to Sue Bailey for locating the photo of The Three Sister, courtesy of the Saskatoon Public Library.

Tellwell Talent
www.tellwell.ca

ISBN
978-0-2288-8048-6 (Paperback)

For Carolyn

Note: The depiction of the "Sisters" as houses used for gambling and prostitution is fictional and created solely for the purposes of this story.

PROLOGUE

As a kid growing up in 1950s Saskatoon, she would ride her bike out to where the city's paved roads ended, and the prairie grasslands began. There, she would gaze across the wide flat expanse to where three empty, weathered clapboard houses stood close together. Everyone referred to them as *The Three Sisters*.

She always wondered how these three abandoned houses had come to be there, standing side by side by side in such an empty landscape. Each were tall and narrow, with two-stories and small-windows, with a few steps leading up to a porch. Each porch landing ran in front of the main entry doorway and continued along to a side door, probably opening into a kitchen or a pantry. Slight structural differences were apparent in each house: window placements, porch railings, and front steps. But she felt it likely that they all were built together, probably at the same time, maybe in 1900 or thereabouts.

Leaving her bike laying in the dirt, she would walk around and in between those old houses but she never crossed their thresholds. Who knew how sound those floorboards were? Or those stairs? But since two of the *Sisters* had lost their front doors, she could see into their entryways and through to the kitchens, where, in one house ... was that a spoon left standing in a coffee cup still in place by the sink? It was like everything was abandoned in a sudden and startling way, or in mid-stir. In the other house she could see up the staircase leading to the upper landing. If she were to have walked up those stairs, she would have found the bedrooms all contained old wooden wardrobes, some with the doors hanging crookedly by a single hinge. Inside, faded garments still hung on the rusted metal hooks, while clothing and women's shoes were heaped in disarray on the beds.

The interiors looked as aged as the exteriors, having been exposed directly to who knew how many extreme prairie seasons. Since most of the windows were gone, she imagined the rooms would fill up with piles of blowing snow in the winter, with the snow becoming banked against the fireplaces and gathering in mounds on the stairs. Icicles probably formed along the mantels or under the door headers, eventually melting and dripping in the spring sun.

Her mother had told her the Sisters had been left in this abandoned state for as long as she could remember. How they appeared to her mother over the years was exactly how they still looked to her, a child in the 1950s. But it is likely that when her mother shared her memories of the houses with her daughter, she probably was unaware of the modest role the "Sisters" had played in the early years of Saskatchewan's settlement.

CHAPTER 1

PYOTR

At thirteen, Pyotr was remarkably fortunate to have escaped a Czarist pogrom. The oppressive Russian government had demanded uniform religious allegiance in addition to the eradication of every synagogue and those who followed the Jewish faith. Every peasant was expected to convert to the Russian Orthodoxy and anyone who opposed the edict was to be wiped from existence. It was after the Cossacks had razed his very small village in the Lviv province in Western Ukraine that Pyotr had made his way to the ocean through Poland in the company of only his grandmother for protection.

Young Pyotr and his *Babushka* had been gathering wildflowers for a village festival when the soldiers arrived. She had hidden the two of them deep inside a hay rick while the plunderers scoured the village and surrounding fields looking for those who may have escaped their sabres. To prevent themselves from crying out, Pyotr and his grandmother had shoved their fists into their mouths. They could hear the Cossacks' horses snorting and stomping as the soldiers circled the hay wagons, stabbing their long swords into some, and setting fire to others.

Hours later, when they were certain the soldiers had moved on, the two of them emerged. What greeted them caused his grandmother to collapse to her knees. As she rocked herself back and forth, Pyotr had held her in his arms while she screamed into her apron. It was close to nightfall, but the silhouettes of the fallen and their mutilated bodies were still visible. When they began to walk about, Pyotr saw his grandmother kneel over the body of one of their neighbours, who was too bloodied and disfigured to be readily identifiable. He watched as she removed the man's belt and wrapped it around his neck, quickly suffocating him to end his suffering. Remnants of fires still burned everywhere; nothing had escaped the attack.

The majority of the villagers had been together in the market hall when the soldiers had arrived. This building and its attached small synagogue had been set on fire and anyone who had tried to run out of the main doors or jumped through the windows had been cut down. Sobbing, Pyotr, and his grandmother moved throughout their destroyed village picking up pieces of clothing and sheepskins, loaves of bread, cheese, and beer. They were each hopeful yet fearful that they would come across their own family members among the bodies laying on the road. But they knew in their hearts that Grandfather Vasily, Pyotr's parents Alexi and Sonia, his sisters Ivanya and Mila, and Uncle Roman had been in the market hall when it was set ablaze. As they made their way to what was left of their *dom,* a neighbour's kitten emerged from a hedge and meowed for food. Pyotr picked it up and tucked it inside his shirt as they continued their survey. No livestock had survived. The oxen and cattle lay slashed and butchered. Every horse had been taken by the invaders.

After Pyotr and his grandmother felt they had scavenged all that would be useful, they began to walk westward toward the ocean. Later that night, they huddled together in a ditch beneath a grove of trees, under the rescued quilts and coverings, with the kitten between them. As his grandmother cradled him, he realized she was crooning the same lullaby to him and his new little furry friend Myushka that she had murmured only hours before to the dying man she had knelt over. Despite the reminder of the carnage, he still found it comforting.

On their trek, scores of other displaced Jews met them, who were on the same journey walking toward the Atlantic through Poland. Pyotr and his grandmother joined dozens of other Jews who would provide them with community and solace. Like the others, Grandmother had sewn jewellery and coins into the hems of her heavily layered undergarments providing them access to food and lodging and eventually paying for their steerage accommodations on a packet ship to Canada. The year was 1890 . . .

******

At the time of their crossing, small border disputes, which had been waging for decades, continued regarding the placement of the dividing line between Canada and the US. A transcontinental rail line to transport troops quickly in case of American encroachment had been the creation of Canada's first prime minister. But America, exhausted by the fallout from its own civil war just twenty years earlier, along with several unsuccessful attempts to establish a military foothold on Canadian soil, decided against expansion north of the forty-ninth parallel. Still, Canadian politicians knew if they were to settle the vast interior of the western provinces, they needed to attract suitable farmers from the predominantly white European farming communities to act as a further deterrent against foreign occupation. Thus, contracts were awarded to land surveyors who systematically mapped out Alberta, Saskatchewan, and Manitoba along strict gridlines allocating ownership of parcels of 160 hectares or a quarter section of land for $10 . . . not exactly free, but almost. The lure of Canadian land was then left to the wild imaginations of thousands of immigrants from Great Britain, Scotland, Ireland, Ukraine, Germany, Poland, Latvia, Lithuania, Norway, Sweden, Finland, Iceland, Belgium, and Russia.

Deeply rooted peasant beliefs led all of these immigrant communities to stare in disbelief at the posters and handbills advertising free land in Canada's interior. How far away **was** Canada? Who gives away farmland freely? Can I truly live without the ruthless demands of a cruel overlord? Will I be free to worship as I want?

******

"Baba, Baba . . . wake up. I have wonderful news. I have such wonderful news."

"Wha . . . Petush . . . what is?"

"We have a chance to sail on a very big ship to America, or Canada, which is just like America I think. I can buy a lot of land for us . . . only a few zloty or rubles or whatever . . . because the government wants to bring us, so the land is . . . now our land. We will travel with a company that will guide us right to our own farm. Our very own farm, Baba! Our prayers . . ."

"Hey you, boy! You can't bring an animal on board."

This decision was quickly vetoed by the ship's purser who knew the value of an adept mouser. Pyotr was only too happy to tuck Myushka's little grey and white head back into his shirt.

"Wait 'til your cat sees the size of the rats down on your deck!"

The month-long crossing soon proved to be more demoralizing for them than just dealing with the rude mocking from the crew members. For Pyotr and his grandmother, the steerage accommodation meant they were placed in the "t'ween deck," which was a deck originally designed to hold cargo. In the early days of immigration, the ships used to convey the immigrants were originally built to carry cargo. Immigrants were now placed in the cargo hold or the "t'ween deck" with flimsy partitions erected between the three-tiered bunks for privacy. To get down to their t'ween deck, Pyotr and his grandmother needed to use a ladder and the passageways that were narrow and steep.

Disease thrived in these squalid conditions. The only ventilation was provided through the hatches to the upper decks, which were kept firmly secured if the seas were rough. Steerage passengers had only buckets to use for seasickness or defecating, which would often spill over in stormy weather. Typhoid, cholera, and smallpox spread unabated.

With respect to eating, it was said, "if a man be more nice than wise," then he would not relish his meal on a packet ship. Watery lukewarm soup, mealy bread, and fetid drinking water comprised most meals. Food was always in short supply. Some ships required passengers to bring their own meagre provisions while others provided a paltry daily amount to keep the passengers from starving. The lack of clean drinking water and rancid food resulted in rampant bouts of dysentery.

Dealing with the overwhelming stench, shared bunks, and limited toilet facilities was difficult enough but not knowing if it was day or night was a constant dismal preoccupation. Pyotr and his grandmother would curl up together on their lower bunk and try to comfort each other between the moments of tear-filled memories and the happier stories of their Ukrainian homeland. Sporadically allowed onto the upper decks, they would gaze out over the deep troughs of waves, spinning daydreams of their new farm, and what they would do with their land. The bright daylight felt intoxicating and in between inhaling the exhilarating salt air, Grandmother would run a bar of damp lye soap over Pyotr's lice-bitten skin to relieve his itching.

At the time of our crossing, the Immigration Act had already been passed by parliament but it was only a half-hearted legislation to try to improve conditions.

New transatlantic regulations did little to eliminate the horrors experienced by those in the lower class accommodations. Our crossing had been arranged by a colonial settlement company that was soon discovered to be guilty of profiteering. Upon our arrival in Quebec City, its representatives were nowhere to be found. We stood on the dock with our fellow immigrants from Russia, all of us realizing that we owned not much more than the clothes on our backs.

******

We remained waiting on the dock as night fell. The busy harbour life was all around with the continuous clanging of bells and blasts from ships' horns. The group was often forced to move out of the way because of the loading and unloading of stores. Massive, heavy ropes were being flung down from the upper decks of incoming ships to be secured around the enormous irons bolted to the docks. Was no one coming to meet us? Finally, the Harbour Master, who had been alerted to our plight, arrived with wagons to carry us to a nearby Sailor's Soup Kitchen.

As we entered the huge facility, the long lines of tables were occupied by hungry men clutching their empty bowls. My grandmother immediately saw what was needed. We all watched, quite dumbstruck, as she handed me her coat and scarf, rolled up her sleeves and started slicing onions. Calling out instructions in Ukrainian, she pointed, organized, and instructed all of us by waving a large knife in the air. No beets were available but with the sacks of recognizable vegetables sitting open at her feet, she began to fill the huge pots with a potato-based soup that I remember to this day. The regular cooks stood rooted in position while she orchestrated all the proceedings. This harbour charity supplied soups, or stews if meat was available, plus bread once a day to scores of hungry mouths. The men needed to provide only a bowl and spoon. And now, it seemed, my grandmother was the newest addition to the kitchen! The cooks appeared only too relieved to concentrate on just their bread tasks. It gave me such pride to see how my grandmother had made this happen.

A bowl of my grandmother's sour borscht soup and a slice of her heavy rye bread was her solution for every problem in life. It soon became our lifeline in those first weeks as we struggled to survive in Quebec City. We were offered free lodgings that first night and for the following eight months in exchange for my Baba's kitchen work. She was diligent in her pursuit of fresh root vegetables and the right spices. She even established a barter system with local hunters for meat. The Sailor's Charity Society located work for me driving a beer wagon and making deliveries up and down the St. Lawrence. Daily, I was tasked with harnessing two of the largest horses I had ever seen to a long beer wagon loaded, stacked, and secured with two dozen small beer kegs. It was a good thing I was young and strong.

The barmaids at my many stops would call out to me, "Bonjour, Chou-Chou!" "Salut Pyotr!" or "Allo, Ruskie!"

Then they would make kissing sounds in the air. I liked it but they also scared me.

Since Baba's money had been stolen by the settlement company, it took us almost two full years to gather enough for the needed farming supplies and to purchase our quarter section. The government would provide free transportation on the Canadian Pacific Railway from Montreal across the southern prairies to our homestead site in Saskatchewan. Such a word! Homesteading! So much better than just "farming."

The government representative who came to see us explained through a translator where we would be homesteading. For our first year we were to build a makeshift shelter out of cut pieces of sod, dirt squares with the grass still in place. He explained that "soddies" were what the prairie farmers were called in the beginning. Sod? Soddies? Dirt squares? With the grasses still attached? He continued to explain the sod shelter was what we would live in until we could build a permanent house . . . or, if we had trees, we could build a log house.

Baba and I tried not to look at each other as we listened, even though the skepticism must have been evident on our faces. Not have trees? We would be allowed three years to build that permanent structure and a barn, and to have cultivated a specified area. Additionally, we needed to dig a well and have purchased a cow or a pig and six chickens. But before our adventure could begin we first needed to make our way to Montreal.

As we sat across from each other on our beds that night, we looked at the photo on the pamphlet of the "Soddy" and his family. Did they look happy? Who knew? Perhaps our dreams were too big. We knew it would take many months to feel at home. But we also knew we would be homesteading alongside our fellow Russian neighbours. We had travelled this far together, across an ocean, and we all would soon be building ourselves a new life in what our government representative called the Palliser Triangle of south central Saskatchewan. After we blew out our candle, we both lay in the dark trying to absorb all this new information.

"Petrush," Baba said, "what do you think . . . if we have dirt sod above our heads, I could plant wildflowers in the grass. Wouldn't that be the most beautiful roof? What a site, seeing a little sod house with flowers in bloom all over the roof. How very pretty in the bright sunshine."

******

Baba and I, along with three of the families from our ship stood on the Montreal railway platform with piles and piles of our assembled gear. Our friends spoke a mix of Russian and Ukrainian but that had never stopped us from feeling connected. We had gravitated toward each other during our crossing and felt a kinship that hardly needed words.

Leaving Montreal aboard our train was an exceptionally turbulent experience. Just standing on the railway platform trying to account for all our belongings, equipment, and livestock was nerve wracking. Everything was so strange. Fortunately, our new settlement company had provided an interpreter who was to travel with us as far as what was called the Lakehead. From there, we would carry on unaccompanied. It would be several days before we would disembark and head into the Saskatchewan prairie to locate our designated quarter section. Baba and I tried to focus our energies on calming our nerves. Besides gazing out the windows at the passing landscape, we spent our time sharing food and memories with our fellow homesteaders. We all had so many questions about our futures.

I was still experiencing night terrors. The scenes of the mutilation and destruction of my wonderful family filled my mind at odd times. Sometimes a smell would trigger a feeling and I would be instantly transported back to that day. Sometimes it was triggered by simply hearing a group of women laughing. Baba and I had been left with nothing, absolutely nothing, to remember our family members by except for our memories. Baba still mourned the unfortunate loss of a treasured necklace that she had received at her own wedding from her husband, my Grandfather Vasily.

But this train ride afforded us the time we needed to share our stories with the others. We constantly talked about our villages and families. We frequently watched each other fall into a tearful silence, which was only lessened by resurrecting a funny story or a folk song. Our four families all had experienced a similar cruel heartbreak so we consoled each other by describing the memorials we would build on our new land to help carry our deceased loved ones in our hearts forever.

Sharing this time with Jakub and his sister Julia, Ivan and Anna plus Mikhail and Maia was made more poignant when I would watch them with their children. I imagined my own little sisters sitting on Baba's lap or on the train's wooden benches, with their noses pressed up against the windows. We had all lost so much. Jakub and his sister had watched their parents die when their farm was overrun by the invaders. Ivan and Mikhail were each forced to pay crushing taxes to unscrupulous overlords. Finally, unable to make the payments they had been forced to consider conscription into armies that would have left their wives and children destitute.

******

When we reached the point of our prairie disembarkation, everything came crashing in on me with a sudden impact once again. I was always surprised that I was the one yearning for my long dead family and our little village in Ukraine, while my resilient grandmother showed nothing but a joyful face for what lay before us.

It took us almost an hour to unload all our livestock, equipment, and supplies. Before we left Montreal, Baba had found an inexpensive coal and wood stove for sale and had insisted it would heat our newly constructed sod house beautifully. It probably weighed a ton, but Baba recognized her needs and I loved making her happy. But all I could think about now was our poor oxen, having to haul a massive iron cooker for miles into the Saskatchewan wilderness.

The confusion felt overwhelming as we sorted through our belongings. We watched each other and without much conversation we yoked our oxen, harnessed the horses, tethered the cattle, loaded furniture, food, trunks, baskets, pitchforks, pails, shovels, and family members into our wagons. How did we appear to the other people who stood on the platform? Had they arrived just to stare at us? It occurred to me later that they just may have been waiting for a train.

We spoke hesitantly in English and the French that we had learned in Eastern Canada would be of no use to us here. But one man stepped forward and offered his hand. His English was as bad as mine, yet we all appreciated his smiling face. Together with his friend they gestured for us to show them our homesteading papers, so they knew in what direction we needed to head. There was a survey map posted on the wall inside the rail station. We crowded around it and tried to make sense of what we were looking at. We understood from their gestures that it would take us over two weeks of travelling overland to reach our sites. At least we had each other, my Baba and me, as well as the other families.

We slept under our wagons for those first nights on the prairie. I looked down at my "little mouse" nestled in the cozy blankets. Baba scratched her behind her ears. Myushka's first two years of life had involved an overland walk to the Atlantic, an arduous ocean crossing, a daily gallop up and down the Gaspé delivering beer, a move from Quebec City to Montreal, and most recently a

900-mile train ride into Saskatchewan's Palliser Prairie Region. My tiny kitten was now a large cat who still insisted on spending most of her daylight hours living inside my shirt. She was really too large to accommodate, positioned as she liked to be around my waist. Besides, it was unbelievably hot as we travelled to our homestead sites and the mosquitoes were unrelenting. But, if Myushka was happy and purring, I was happy and purring too.

CHAPTER 2

LIZZIE AND MARY

My older sister, Mary, refused to go anywhere without me and would create a horrid ruckus if there was any threat of our being separated. Actually, Mary was my mother and knew instinctively we must never be apart. As I grew older, she thought we appealed more to the sympathies of others as siblings, rather than as a parent and child. By the time I was eight, we did look like we could possibly be siblings. Although she was a tiny woman and appeared meek, it was all a trick. Anyone who underestimated her immediately felt her tongue.

Mary had not received much formal education past knowing her letters and how to add numbers, but she was a keen observer. And that skill compensated a lot for the missed schooling. She had listened intently to how words were enunciated, ever so perfectly, by her ladyship and had practised a very erect posture, which seemed to her to be the mark of a true lady. When she began to notice the small signs of admiration from his Lordship, she told me she knew immediately what he wanted. She had no intention, however, of having her good fortune as a newly hired junior chambermaid compromised.

When my mother was fifteen, she had left the Liverpool Paupers' Workhouse to take up a place in an elegant household as a junior chambermaid. In her newly appointed chambermaid position, she had been assigned spacious servant's quarters and told me, so excitedly that she had felt a swell of pride and gratitude each time she donned her beautiful chambermaid's livery. But, six months later she had been forced to return to the pauper workhouse because she had found herself expecting a child. When her bulging pregnant belly had become impossible to hide, the head housekeeper in his Lordship's mansion had promptly dismissed her. There was no sympathy or understanding given to the circumstances leading up to her condition; the fault was said to be entirely hers.

Not to be intimidated by the snobbish pretensions of his Lordship who had so forcibly molested her one morning when she was sent to change his bed linens, she presented herself on the sidewalk in front of his prestigious bank. With the promise of a daily repeat performance until they could negotiate a settlement for herself and his unborn child. My mother eventually bargained for the right to a private room in the parish's pauper workhouse for the two of us plus the additional princely sum of ten pounds per year.

On March 15, 1885, my mother and I stepped off a ship from the White Star Steamship Line out of Liverpool, onto the docks of Quebec City, with a small trunk containing everything we owned. She always said she knew in that instance she would never see England again. All she felt in that moment was fear and isolation.

I was only a young child at the time, with my "sister" in circumstances that had left us quite destitute. She told me her memory of arriving in a strange land, where the welcoming priest spoke only French, would stay with her forever.

MARY

I always felt so blessed to have wonderful teeth. As I grew older, they came in straight, regular, and white. I was also gifted with a bountiful head of hair plus even comely features which, although a blessing, often proved problematic.

Like my Lizzie, I too was born in a Liverpool workhouse. Both my parents, recently arrived potato famine immigrants from Ireland, sadly died of consumption shortly after I was born. They had arrived at Liverpool's harbour aboard one of the many "coffin ships" carrying destitute Irish immigrants to what was supposed to be a better life. They had travelled on an open deck packet steamer to Liverpool where they waited in the basements of quayside buildings for transport to North America. When it was discovered that they were both riddled with tuberculosis, they were prevented from boarding their designated ship and ended up in the paupers' workhouse where I was eventually born.

If it had not been for the kindness of my most wonderful benefactress, Mistress Florence, I dread to think what would have happened to me. It was often said how Miss Florence Pennyweight, as a patron of The Liverpool Paupers' Workhouse Society, would visit the premises to ensure the safekeeping, hygiene, and health of its charges. One day as she toured the nursery, her eyes fell upon me as I sat upright in my small crib, a sweet cherubic angel. I came to know this "spinster lady of powerful resolve" well. Over the years, she incorporated a rudimentary school program into our workhouse apprenticeships. She volunteered herself frequently to try and instruct groups of unruly children who had absolutely no interest in learning. She told me herself that she had been instrumental in persuading legislators to require workhouses to offer basic literacy. This, she said, was to ensure that all pauper apprentices would be able to read and sign their own indenture papers.

The Three Sisters

I was fifteen when she championed me, her "star," as a chambermaid within his Lordship's house. It proved to be quite a feather in my cap (and hers, I expect). It was only six months later that I had to reappear on that very same workhouse doorstep and see the sad disappointed face of my wonderful Mistress Florence standing before me. I knew it was with great sadness that she enveloped me in her strong embrace. From then on, I always had a feeling that she had intervened in the destruction of the private reputation of his Lordship's household, which had so uncharitably turned me out. His Lordship was also soundly castigated amongst his fellow philanthropic club members who always wished to present themselves as benefactors rather than common, vulgar users.

Following the birth of my sweet daughter Lizzie, it was easy for me to undertake the tedious chore of "working the junk." Cartloads of cut pieces of ships' rope were delivered to the workhouses to be untwined and in their unravelling, turned into caulking. The shipyards of Plymouth, Bristol, and Liverpool provided tons and tons of junk, or oakum, a job everyone hated because of its monotonous repetition. But, for me, I could place wee Lizzie in a laundry basket at my feet while I fiddled the piles and piles of oakum that appeared to be endless. Untwisted, the yarns were separated and reduced to shreds by hand. And by rubbing the rope piece against my apron, it became what could be used for caulking, its original intention. There was nothing straining about this task, but it was tiresome, and I made various attempts to evade it. However, in undertaking this job, I was able to closely supervise the first six years of Lizzie's life.

I had no say when I was sent to a weaving factory to work. It was a relief to get away from the oakum, I grant you, but I was forced to leave my sweet Lizzie unsupervised to work the junk on her own. I was first placed in the workhouse laundry and textile section. Glove and hat maker factories were usually housed in the same industrial buildings as the loom and laundry factories so perhaps I could work my way into a glove and millinery apprenticeship. Because the workhouses fed local industry, an apprentice could earn about fifty quid a year for the poorhouse. Until then, I was tasked with carding, spinning, and stitching. It really mattered nought where I went as long as Lizzie and I were together at day's end.

"What was your hour in school about today?" I would ask her as we met for evening tea.

"No school. Picked oakum all day. Hard on my fingers, Mummy. I so hate it."

I knew because of Lizzie's age that she had the possibility of being placed in the cotton and wool factories at the "gins." The engines were ferocious in their destruction of childhood dreams. Everyone knew that. My Lizzie was of an age when that could happen. Unions were slowly acknowledging their opposition to the placement of children at the cotton gins. But the adults who ran the mills were entirely indifferent to the plight of their child workers. It was a rough working environment and accidents happened. So, when the Bernardo Foundation proposed our sponsorship in the Home Children Program, I chose Canada for us, rather than Australia or South Africa. It was at this point that I notified his Lordship that he need not further supply us with our yearly stipend. I felt his payment and our connection to him needed to end. Our passage was already in place, courtesy of the Bernardo Foundation who would indenture us to a textile factory in Canada until our debt was cleared.

Unbeknownst to all the agencies, over the years since her birth, Lizzie and I had acquired a substantial amount in English pounds, which we had hidden away in cotton pockets sewn into our petticoats.

Lizzie and I were lucky to be placed together in a fine linens and millinery factory upon our arrival in Montreal. We had originally disembarked in Quebec City but before we had continued our journey, the Salvation Army took over our contract from the Bernardo Foundation. They soon determined I was at least eighteen and too old to be indentured. We had stated on our entry papers that

Lizzie's age was twelve although she was in fact two years younger. But that gave her only six years to pay off her immigration debt. Happily, for us, public opinion was beginning to turn against the Home Children Program. An editorial in the 1890 Canadian Manufacturer copy stated:

> *A greater outrage never was perpetrated upon a community than that controlled by Dr. Barnardo, of London, whose great aim seems to be to gather up all the waifs and offscourings of the slums of that great city and to dump as many of them upon this country as it can possibly receive.*

Did these new attitudes benefit Lizzie and me? At the time, I saw no benefit. What I did know was that I was offered a position of authority after only a few weeks following our arrival in Montreal. We had been originally assigned positions at the wool looms. Our time spent doing the same labour in Liverpool had given us a leg-up. Yes, it was repetitive work, but we took great delight in not having to scramble around on the floor like the small children underneath our feet who had to sweep up stray pieces of wool, threads, and fabric ends.

It seems, at the time of our arrival, the factory workers of Eastern Canada were beginning to organize with other factory workers across the country to demand better working conditions as well as higher wages and reduced working hours. So, I was greatly surprised to be offered a new position as an Authorizing Overseer. The man I was to replace was leaving to become a labour organizer for the Unified Factory Workers of Quebec and Ontario. From the angry scowls on the faces of my fellow loom workers, who sat glaring at me over their weavings, I knew it was important to decline this questionable promotion. And from the look on the overseer's face, I guessed my dimples were one of the reasons for my promotion. Sooner, rather than later, he would come to collect his reward. No thank you. Besides, I knew how dangerous it was to jump the queue.

LIZZIE

Two years I have now spent at the floor loom. I thank my increasing height and long legs for allowing me to sit before the threads. But the lighting is poor at my station and this factory has no ventilation. My schooling has been sporadic, but we try to fit nightly reading into our evening routine. Mary, I can now proudly announce, is to be called Mother or Mama and is no longer referred to as my older sister. This transformation has come about largely due to the strong women my mother has met at

Mrs. Finnerty's boarding house for respectable women. We love our two cheerful rooms (with a little fireplace!) in this warm and welcoming household.

I have watched my mother grow confident in the joyous camaraderie of strong independent women. I have really no one my age to be with as a friend besides my mother. The factory has scores of children in various jobs, but in my area of the textile mill they are mostly boys and I have no interest in their stupid games. It's the boys who throw the shuttles on the large looms. I know how boredom can set in and accidents can happen easily, like pinched fingers and loose clothing being caught. But they will never be promoted because they take nothing seriously and all too frequently cause accidents. They do make good dinner toters though. They are good at running meals to the loom workers so there's a minimum of production time lost.

I am hoping to be promoted to a spinner position. Now that power looms are being brought in to replace the big floor looms, they need workers to walk the long aisles, brushing lint from the machines and watching the spools for breaks. Once a break is found, they must stop the machine and tie the ends together. The hardest part of the job is that spinners are on their feet working eight- or ten-hour shifts in an extremely noisy environment, six days a week.

The machine looms and their loud mechanical sounds seem to appeal more to the boys who say the noises sound like hammer and tong clangs from the blacksmith forges and farriers' barns. The boys are also excited to be trained as Doffers. They get to climb onto the machines to replace the bobbins. When all the machines are running, no one can engage in normal levels of conversation; we all yell at each other like crazed fools and make exaggerated hand gestures. As well, we always stuff our ears with spit and wool bits to shut out the noises.

MARY

I have now been placed in the needle trades shop below Lizzie's floor. An extremely heavy droning sound comes through the upstairs floorboards when all the machine looms are started up in the morning. The sound is like a gigantic nest of angry wasps. I am being trained for fine needlework finishing and am paid for individual piecework. My specialties are lace trimmings and silk embellishments. Banks of electric sewing machines are being installed and the production level of the finished work is organized on a daily quota per worker.

The new political upstart, William Lyon Mackenzie King, is making a point of touring the garment district sweatshops of Montreal to report to the current Canadian government about working environments and trade practices. I am spending Sunday afternoons discussing the inequities in our area of the garment industry. Forbidden to talk to other workers while on the job, I have begun inviting co-workers for Sunday afternoon tea. Mrs. Finnerty was slow to support these efforts for discussion but eventually came around. Now, the rooming house parlour often is abuzz with disgruntled female pieceworkers sharing the need for improvements in their working conditions.

Women, I have always known, are more vulnerable in the garment industry. We are regularly exploited in a variety of situations unlike the men who are considered to be more skilled and given the positions of cutters, trimmers, and pressers. For example, I know an identification system for finished products is needed throughout the garment industry. European women who dominate the needle trades, have specific grievances. Too many poorly finished piecework items are wrongly identified. I have taught them to say, "That's not my job" in English as a memorized response since they don't have the language skills to argue further. Harassment from taskmaster bosses often end in pay cuts or hours lost due to minor infractions like needing a bathroom break outside of normal times, opening a laundry window to clear the starch-filled air, or not filling a weekly quota because of slowness. Some supervisors use stopwatches and implement speed-ups when orders increase. Armed with a list of needed improvements in our working conditions, I am planning on presenting myself as a spokeswoman, however naively I see my ability to offer representation. My intention is to meet with the factory employers and bargain in good faith.

******

My employers, of course, are incensed with being asked to change their business practices and my list of suggestions has been immediately discarded. They claim complete autonomy in operating decisions. They alone set the wages and claim the right to hire and fire. I am immediately branded a troublemaker and blacklisted by the time I leave the building. My Lizzie is also dismissed because of our association.

That night, walking back to our rooming house, both Lizzie and I feel surprisingly light-hearted.

"Quite nice to stick it to that horrible little weasel-faced Mr. Simpkins with his wandering hands," Lizzie offers. "Good for you, Mama."

"I wholeheartedly agree. Only, he'll walk into a job tomorrow while we won't."

"This is the perfect time for us to dig into our hidden petticoat resources, don't you think?"

CHAPTER 3

ALBERT

Albert, at eighteen was a third-generation descendant of the United Empire Loyalists who had fled the US for their support of Britain following the American War of Independence in 1776. He is a child of privilege and the establishment. His father is a newspaper publisher turned lumber baron and considered landed gentry. Their family's arrival from one of the thirteen colonies following the American Revolution demonstrated evidence of their loyalty to the British King, George III, and sealed their position in the society of Upper Canada. Albert's ancestors, and all those who were proud to place UE after their names, were granted 200 acres of land by the Canadian government to reward their loyalty.

As Albert was growing up, his family greatly admired his intellectual pursuits but worried constantly about his unusual, anti-social behaviour. Albert had developed a deep fascination for everything in his surroundings. He was intrigued by machines and their workings. He gathered rocks and minerals and studied the geological formations of nearby cliffs. He would spend hours in the branches of a tree, sitting stock still near a nest, hoping for the return of the mother bird. He devoted weeks to reading about the movements of bees and their pollination patterns, or to study the habits of migrating ducks. He studied architecture and assisted in building the Italianate facade alongside his father's hired carpenters for their family home in Upper Canada.

His family knew Albert's time was well spent with all his reading, newspaper articles, and encyclopedias, but his insular, bookish behaviour was not the problem. The problem was Albert demonstrated a frightening lack of ability for conversation or social interaction. Even with his sympathetic father and sister, Albert said his tongue would suddenly feel so swollen that he was incapable of speech. All his efforts resulted in an excruciating stammer. He was rendered so incapacitated when asked to explain an observation or theory that he would stumble from the room shaking uncontrollably and sweating profusely. Regular schooling was a torment; Albert's doctors were at a loss. Albert's mother had never been patient with him, and her reactions had always been critical, filling him with shame.

Thankfully, he had a warm and supportive father and older sister. Despite her recent marriage, and the birth of twins, his sister played an active role in thwarting Mother's misguided attempts to "fix" Albert. She and Albert's father prevented Mother from following the advice of several physicians who advocated invasive mouth and tongue surgeries as solutions. Neither would allow it. Mother's next step was to have special leather and metal devices constructed to restrict Albert's jaw movement. Again, Father and Albert's sister rejected any solution that prevented the movement of his mouth and tongue as suitable therapies. They knew instinctively the ideas advanced by medicine at the time were invasive and destructive.

It was Albert's sister who hit upon the paper and pencil assist for easier communication. Perhaps it would not solve the stammer immediately, but it would provide Albert with the much-needed time and space to collect his thoughts before attempting to speak.

"Albie, look here, Sweetheart. I know it's very slow, but I think you'll develop speed with your pencil. People are essentially good and will want to help. Your responses of course will be much slower but anyone you're talking to will be only too happy to wait. You'll see. If you can approach each exchange with a smile on your face and maintain eye contact, you will soon have a gradual success."

First attempts were not as successful as he would have wished. He felt completely mortified. However, after daily practice with his father and sister for over a year, he began to feel he could venture farther afield and begin to "speak" with strangers. He carried his small pad of paper and pencil in his left breast pocket and began to make a bit of a ceremony in removing them. Albert found a slow and steady gaze plus a friendly smile set the tone for a relaxed mood. It was said Albert's focused listening skills were the key to his success. And to that end, his father began to recognize his ability in negotiating lumber contracts where paper and pencil bids were commonplace. Albert would happily spend the next year accompanying his father throughout Upper and Lower Canada contracting timber resources. He was beginning to feel relief from the years of endured tortures. His reddening cheek blush would always remain, but he was told his high colouring was quite attractive.

As he gained confidence and felt the admiration for his efforts growing, he wondered if he could explore other opportunities outside his family's influence. He was drawn to ideas that encouraged the exploration of a larger Canada. It was also a chance to escape his mother's constant negative scrutiny. He knew his father would support his need for independence. His sister would also encourage him in this regard; plus, she was busy with her new family duties. How he would miss his little twin nieces; he loved being their Uncle Albie. He was, after all, the only adult who refrained from telling them what to do.

He read with great interest about the completion of the transcontinental Canadian Pacific Railway. And with that last spike being driven, extensive travel and settlement of Canada's interior was burgeoning. The government was seeking qualified land surveyors to divide the three interior provinces into quarter sections. They were to follow a strictly numbered grid system and plant long marked pegs deeply into the soil to prevent tampering with property boundaries. Trains carrying hundreds of "desirable" farming immigrants from around the world were arriving monthly from Montreal. These trains travelled through the Lakehead to the massive dispersal railway yards outside Fort Winnipeg. From there, most homesteading groups took one of two routes to reach their new land. They either boarded the Canadian Pacific Railway line and travelled parallel to the forty-ninth parallel or, they signed onto wagon trains and followed the deeply rutted, overland Carleton Trail heading diagonally from the Red River area of Southern Manitoba to Fort Edmonton.

Albert became very caught up in the romance of this huge pioneering effort. He marvelled at the descriptions of the wooden-wheeled Red River carts and their caterwauling screech and squeal while being pulled along by oxen. He could imagine himself with all his surveying equipment, mapping out a designated area of the prairie land, planting the stakes to mark each corner boundary for a quarter section of land. He then pictured a newly arrived pioneer family discovering that very same marked peg. He saw them excitedly asking each other if the numbers and letters matched? After checking and rechecking, and rechecking again, they would discover that yes, where they now stood was indeed their new land. Their land! Their own land! With certificates and proof of purchase in hand, they would whoop, dance, and kiss each other's tear-streaked faces. Albert wanted to play a part in that fantasy.

June 10, 1886

My Dearest Papa,

It is only because of your constant love and support that I dare entertain the notion of striking out on my own. I've read the requirements for becoming certified as a land surveyor and have made an application to the Canadian Dominion Land Surveyance Company for apprenticeship licensing. The compass, the chain, and the transit are now to become my new acquaintances and I know, will prove to be loyal companions. Papa, I am so grateful for your constant encouragement in helping me understand the challenges of advanced mathematics. The engineering requirements for surveying land feel completely within my ability and knowing I am capable, fills me with confidence and contentment. I will be doing something I love.

I will always do you proud, dear Papa. You have provided me with two decades of your exemplary parenting and I look to you constantly for continued guidance. I will write often and tell you of my great adventures!

Your most loving son,

Albert

******

June 10, 1886

My Sweet Sister,

I am off on such an adventure. Father will explain my new decisions. The two of you have always championed my efforts and without your constant hurrahs, rippings, and good shows I never would have felt capable of kicking off the traces to head into Canada's interior.

Give both of your precious offspring an enormous hug from their adoring uncle. I will write constantly. Mother tells me you are expecting a new child who will be born in early spring of next year. How marvellous.

My fondest affection,

Albie

******

June 10, 1886

Mother,

I am leaving on a grand adventure.

Albert

******

August 30, 1886

My Dearest Family,

I have spent two months establishing myself here in Regina. I am now most fortunate in being placed as a surveyor's apprentice to a Mr. Henry Kirkham, from Parry Sound, Ontario. I have heard wonderful things about this man. He is to become my mentor and teacher until my preliminary fieldwork is completed here in Saskatchewan's capital. If all proceeds as I plan, my final surveying certification will be awarded at the end of next year.

You would like him, Father. His manner reminds me of you. When I'm feeling memories of home overwhelm me, I am able to confide in Henry as I once did with you.

Henry and I met in the large commercial centre here in Regina. I was then introduced to the impressive Federal Dominion Lands organization for which I am now employed. I am told I will be returning to these Land Registry offices every three months to transfer written information from our field books onto the legal documentation needed to be given to the proper government offices who in turn give them to the homesteaders. The entire system is overseen by many eyes at every level to ensure accuracy.

It's incredible for me to realize I am playing a part in this unique checkerboard system that will cover 200 million acres and is the world's largest survey grid system. Henry tells me when all three prairie provinces are mapped out, 1.25 million quarter section homesteads will have been created. I can hardly believe a number that large!

Henry makes me feel such pride for my chosen profession. He has instilled in me a deep respect for establishing the boundaries of land ownership. Using the engineer's tools of the transit and chain plus my knowledge of trigonometry, I feel I have gravitated toward a rewarding professional life.

Henry and I are at present gathering all our surveying equipment, horses and two wagons, tenting supplies plus food, chairs, tables, wash basins, and cooking pots to be able to head out to our designated area in Southern Saskatchewan. The heavy snows will begin in late November so we are told our departure to the Palliser Triangle should not be delayed.

Family, I am not certain any letters can reach you until I return to our headquarters, but I will write often to give you a weekly record of our progress.

A warm embrace to all of you. Uncle Albie says hello to my two small cabbages, (soon to be three!).

Albie

******

May 30, 1887

Dear Wonderful Family,

The heartiest of sincere congratulations to you, exceptional sister, for birthing your sweet little Albert. I am so touched you chose my name for our new family addition. I will always do my best to be a suitable role model for my young namesake.

In the many months since Henry Kirkham and I departed from Regina's central survey offices, much has happened and how my horizons have expanded!

You would hardly recognize my appearance as I have changed my traditional three-piece tweed suit and white shirt with those awful, stiff detachable celluloid collars, for the garb of a hardy land surveyor: heavy canvas pants and work boots, long underwear (which doubles as sleeping apparel, and very necessary in winter I'm told), flannel shirt (long-sleeved for protection against mosquitoes), slouchy felt hat, and neck square. My hair is now almost to my shoulders and tied in the back by a leather thong. Henry says I look more like a pioneer than an actual pioneer.

My surveying skills, I am told, are becoming increasingly more thorough and accurate. I watch Henry in his careful calculations despite the occasional hilly or forested terrain. Every day is a new adventure and surprisingly, for such flat land, the topography changes constantly. Even the demands of precise record keeping are interesting to me. I feel so rewarded knowing how vital my contribution is.

The Saskatchewan prairies are amazing to me, and the Palliser Triangle has such history! Chief Sitting Bull crossed into this very region as a place of refuge after Custer's slaughter in the Battle of Little Bighorn. He was finally forced back over the forty-ninth parallel onto American soil along with the many loyal Sioux who followed him. Their hunger, starvation, and an inhospitable winter environment proved too much.

Henry (what a teacher!) is such a wealth of knowledge about early Saskatchewan. He seems to have a kinship with the land itself and its vast array of immigrant settlers. He is the best surveying partner I could ever have imagined. In the last twenty-five years, he has laid out the grid lines for almost all the land in Northern Saskatchewan and seems to know most of the early homesteaders in that region. He loves to revisit them after they've established themselves to oversee their homesteading probationary period. They all welcome him as one of their own.

The first Saskatchewan homesteaders came off the Carlton Trail, he said, and were composed largely of German Hutterites and Scandinavians. Homesteads were also granted to Veterans and nurses of the Boer Wars as well as the Métis who had lost their land in the Riel Rebellion of '85 against the North West Mounted Police.

But things have now changed for Henry and me.

When we began the South Saskatchewan Palliser survey, I felt a lot of Henry's disillusion and disappointment as we viewed the land before us. It appeared devoid of much of the necessary agricultural ingredients to sustain homesteading. And yet, it is presently being offered to the homesteaders as the answer to their prayers.

Henry has previously experienced the wealth of farming possibilities in Northern Saskatchewan, so he knows what he's talking about regarding the lack of possibilities for the Southern Palliser. From his readings, he tells me the Palliser Region is an extension of the great interior central desert which runs from Texas up through the Dakotas into the south central area of Saskatchewan. This was the area the buffalo followed until their migration routes were interrupted by the railroad tracks, which run along the forty-ninth. I agree with Henry's observation that these disruptions to the important natural patterns are being slowly revealed as the west is becoming settled.

Much affection,

Albert

CHAPTER 4

PYOTR

Our four wagons travelled slowly north through land that looked empty of cultivation potential. My stoic grandmother sat quietly beside me while I drove the oxen, but I know she silently wept. Even Myushka trembled at the sight of the many gophers and prairie dogs, which popped their little heads up out of their burrows as we moved past. We stared straight ahead, neither of us talking or looking at each other. What we saw were stretches of cactus, shrubs, and short grasses amid an endless sea of sand dunes. We still had at least seven more days before reaching our homestead sites so hopefully the land will become greener. We push aside notions of the Canadian government selling us poor land. Why would they pay for our train transportation to only provide us with homesteads unsuitable for cultivation? Our four families have purchased one entire section of land, 640 acres, and where the four corners of the sections meet is where we will erect our first sod homes.

Thankfully, after the second week, our wagon train gradually moves into land that is more forested. From a distance we can see a line of treetops. As we come closer, the tall stands of birch, alder, and pine are now thicker, and the air feels fresher and crisper. When we encounter what we identify as the North Saskatchewan River from our map, we keep it on our left and travel northeast in the direction of its flow. We know fording this river would be hazardous until we reach a stretch where the river shallows considerably and sandbars emerge. We feel almost instinctively that we are near our markers and with trembling hands we take out our compasses and documents. It is possible we are standing on our actual homestead land at this very moment. When we finally locate the survey marker post and indeed identify the numbers from the survey charts, it becomes our favourite memory. We relive it constantly. How Baba thrashed through the trees calling out, *Where are you, my long wooden marker? Where are you? . . . oh, Pyotr. Here it is! I've found it!*

******

Our four families spend the following two weeks walking our entire quarter sections, marvelling at our good fortune. Our closest neighbours, two widowed women named Constance and Anna tell our families, through an odd series of pantomimed gestures, that a new rail spur is to be built about two miles east, which will mean our crops can eventually be transported to market.

At night we still pull our wagons into a circle and sleep beneath them. The surrounding forest supplies all the campfire wood we will ever need, plus a plentiful amount of wild game. Rabbits, deer, and antelope are everywhere as well as ducks and pheasants. We talk of where to locate our new sod structures and the eventual future log houses we will build. We have heard the river freezes in the winter, so maybe then, we will be able to dance and slide on frozen water. We spin many fantasies. Although it is late spring, we know we have plenty of time to prepare for the snow.

******

I am now seventeen and feel the eyes of women on me. But since Baba is my special girl, it is for her that I spend each day fashioning mud and clay bricks for our first sod house. We decide rather than cutting bricks out of the soil we will dig muddy clay from the riverbanks. The next step is to pound this mixture into wooden forms.

When mixed with grasses and left to dry in the sun, the bricks are almost completely intact when we push them from their moulds.

Our new little sod house has two rooms, and its flat roof is covered with grass sod into which Baba happily plants her wildflowers. Our furniture in the main room consists of a willow bed frame with a roped latticed support for her stuffed wool and goose down mattress and a table with two chairs. Some religious prints plus our enormous cooking range completes the main room. Near the cooktop, Baba keeps her pantry items on two shelves. We also have wooden pegs for our sheepskin coats, jackets, and other clothing.

Our second room is for Baba's setting hen and her chicks because it will be too cold in the winter for an outdoor enclosure. This room also has an exterior door opening into a small lean-to for our sheep and two horses. I have begun to chop firewood for sale to supply us with winter provisions such as kerosene, matches, molasses, needles, thread, candles, and animal feed.

Often, I watch my grandmother as she walks out several strides from our sod structures to view them from a distance with their brightly coloured rooftops. We even have blooms on the roof of our small outhouse. They each have a dirt floor and once a week Baba smears a thin coating of mud, which dries and hardens. Sweeping those dried mud floors is one of her great pleasures. I have built benches against the exterior walls, so visitors have a place to sit. I have lined the door frames and windows with wood slabs cut lengthwise and have hung carved doors and windows.

I am slow to realize I have this building skill but soon realize it is what I had absorbed as a young boy watching my father Alexei and Grandfather Vasily back in our village in Ukraine. So, I lend any of my spare time to helping the other families. Mikhail, Jakub, Ivan, and I have discussed how to share our talents for construction and farming while the women will assist each other with childcare and domestic chores. Our four sod houses are now only a ten-minute walk apart and are separated by stands of trees. We have each other close by but we also have privacy.

CHAPTER 5

LIZZIE

Our arrival at Toronto's rail station is not the disembarkation I feared. We have entered a huge bustling city filled with bicycles, horse drawn carts, and automobiles jamming the streets. I know before we moved that Mama was sad to leave our Montreal rooming house and worried that we would be entering a colonial backwater in moving to Toronto. Happily, this is not the case. We even read about a local paper company being the first to sell rolls of toilet tissue, a revolutionary idea for Victorian Toronto. Previously, people used rags, leaves, wood shavings, hay, or corn cobs. Mama is so pleased with this news because she loathes anything that reminds her of poverty or her early life in Liverpool.

We moved from Montreal because of her workplace advocacy, so she is now determined to enter the seamstress trade of Toronto with a greater understanding of her need for discretion. At this time in Toronto, union activities are becoming more commonplace and factory owners are being forced to negotiate hours, conditions, and wages. She discovers the successful Toronto Printer's Strike of 1872 has gradually initiated a movement that enables workers to safely join unions for hour and wage negotiations. But even twenty years on, factory life in the garment industry is still brutal and we all know it.

MARY

Lizzie and I find a most suitable rooming house located in a pretty area off Yonge Street. We have two rooms with easy street access. Only a few steps further and we can ride on the newly installed system of electric streetcars. Twice we have ridden the streetcar to the end of the line along the waterfront route, which is great fun. It appears downtown Toronto in 1904 is undergoing extensive rebuilding after a major fire destroyed many of its crowded factories and tenements. The city is determined to rebuild these structures alongside newly created scenic areas to provide green spaces for picnicking families on Sunday, their one day off work.

It is only after viewing the progressive state of affairs in Toronto that I decided to pursue the idea of enrolling Lizzie in school. Turn-of-the-century Toronto has legislators who are remarkably modern about a whole range of social needs. Their programs target the prohibition of liquor as well as the suffrage movement. But for me, their one great advancement is the introduction of free public education. No longer just for the children of wealthy parents, schooling could be for the general population. Lizzie is now almost thirteen and at least two inches taller than me. She will need some hard persuasion to enter a school setting with much younger (and shorter) students.

"But you didn't even ask me if I wanted to go to school!" she wails in response to my announcement.

"I know, I know. It was a decision I made without consulting you."

"But, why, Mama? I can read and do numbers so well right now."

"I'll not have you at the machines any longer, Lizzie. It's no life. And that's the end of this nonsense. And you can stop your pouting!"

******

The actual school building in which Lizzie is now attending is an aging structure with a leaking ceiling and a strong smell of mildew. But she seems to love it. She has been assessed at a Grade 6 level, so her height is not such a huge issue. Her teacher is an attractive young woman named Miss Lucy Ambrose.

"And, Mama, she rides a bicycle to school!"

Life for Lizzie is now quite grand. For me, I return to completing piecework, which puts me back onto the garment factory line. The clothing industry has always been largely concerned with driving their production costs ever lower so demands for increased hourly pay and improved working conditions were areas in which I knew to tread cautiously.

I presented my skills with the electric sewing machine and almost immediately secure employment with the T. Eaton Company Ltd. In my building alone they have employed over 2,000 seamstresses working electric machines to supply products for their mail order catalogue business as well as their retail trade. Although women far outnumber men in the needle trades, it is women who are in a more precarious position for maintaining their employment. Men are also able to utilize the trade union movement more effectively. I hate it that in the busy seasons that women are expected to work longer hours, only to be the first laid off during the spells of lower orders. I am going to have to learn, however, to keep my opinions to myself. I have returned once again to being treated as a second-class worker.

Our rooming house is near my garment factory, which is filled with immigrant women completing piecework. Walking to my factory every morning, it occurs to me that if I had a machine at home I could turn out skirts, blouses, suits, and topcoats for clothing manufacturers independent of the factory process. I wouldn't really need a factory setting to complete my piecework; I could work directly from home. The manufacturer would provide the fabrics (possibly) and I would supply my own thread, sew up the garments, and deliver the finished articles to either the factory or the garment company. As this idea begins to take root, the purchase of a sewing machine, probably a used treadle, becomes my focus.

I begin with the idea of creating cycling apparel for the athletic woman. Having Lizzie's teacher in mind, I copy an ankle-length, split skirt design from a Parisienne fashion magazine. Purchasing suitable fabrics will be key in creating the right product. This is a look that is being adopted as the symbolic costume for many American suffragettes. Their photos dominate the newspapers and I know before long the women of Toronto will copied it.

I pair my split skirt with a tweed jacket suitably nipped at the waist to still appear feminine. Worn with a tailored blouse and button boots to cover the ankle, it creates a very attractive feminine silhouette. The right hat will take more thought but for now I decide to use a man's style straw boater. The corset? I also need to give that more consideration. A vest? A useful addition.

As soon as I am finished creating this new ensemble, I buy a bicycle.

LIZZIE

When Miss Ambrose told me I had an exceptional mind, I felt my whole-body sail skyward. I knew I would live off those words forever. Now that I'm nearing the final days of Grade 9, the last three years under her tutelage are coming to a close. Next term, I will have the dreaded Miss Gilmore who has a passion only for sentence parsing and penmanship and lacks the romantic inclination to study the great poets and writers of English literature. I take constant comfort in the fact that the beautiful Miss Ambrose will continue to supply me with books from her father's library, which feed my very soul.

Yesterday our class received the year's final marks for all our core subjects, and I was awarded the English Composition prize. It seems I excel at writing, which Mama finds remarkable. My winning entry was a personal biography that I entitled, in very bold letters, **Who Were The People Before Me.** I started with the bits and pieces of the history of Mama's father and mother, Thomas and Elizabeth Dooley, who were potato famine refugees from

The Three Sisters

Ireland and an heirloom silver locket, which my mother still wears daily. I wrote about my birth in a Liverpool workhouse and carried through to my arrival in Lower Canada alongside my exceptional mother. All this writing came easily to me.

Mama has always shared every detail of our journey but from the look in her eyes, I knew Miss Ambrose had very little knowledge of my background. It wasn't that I had always presented a brave face and hidden a great sorrow. Not at all. I just didn't want anything to alter my admiration for Miss Ambrose or change our relationship with any undue sympathy that she might feel for me. And now with this writing accolade under my belt, I am free for most of the summer to ride my new bicycle, an additional scholastic prize from my proud mother.

CHAPTER 6

ALBERT

January 1, 1890

Dearest Family,

Winter has thoroughly descended here on the prairies and all of Saskatchewan is taking shelter beside wood stoves or fireplaces. I am reminded of the deep snows from my childhood and the fun we had making snow angels. Remember when Brute was just a puppy and his crazy reactions to falling snowflakes? Since the banks of snow are about as deep as the wheels on our motor cars and carriages, we venture outdoors with great care. The wind is fierce and sometimes heaps of snow pile up against exit doors, which then takes several bodies and many shovels to open.

It is with the warmest of New Year's thoughts that I wish only good fortune for my loved ones in this coming year. Being away from all of you this past Christmas was a greater hardship than I imagined. I have now been in Saskatchewan for four years. The time has passed quickly but seasonal celebrations remind me how I miss all of you. Henry's family has once again taken me in and made my Christmas truly jolly. He has a wonderful wife and two teenage daughters who kept me entertained and distracted from thoughts of my own family.

My next six months will be spent taking classes in conveyancing and the legal requirements regarding land acquisition. I'm also becoming more familiar with the Saskatchewan prairie lakes and river systems plus the general topography. At this point it is largely only that which I see on maps and charts, so my practical knowledge is lacking. I am beginning to feel Henry's passion for this interior province, to be newly installed in the great Canadian Confederation within the coming decade if the rumours are correct.

Henry's wife and daughters are descendants of early mid-century Hudson Bay Company's Scottish employees and local Indigenous women so his attachment to the land runs deep. It seems so foundational to the strong pioneering spirit of the land. They are the Métis, and Henry's honouring of their heritage is exceptional.

Henry told me of his first sighting of his wife Amelia. He watched her as she walked across a wide stretch of pasture land toward her family's homestead house. Henry was there, on Amelia's father's land, to oversee the first three-year probationary period for establishing ownership of their quarter section. Henry saw Amelia with her thick black, waist length hair blowing in the wind and felt an instantaneous attachment. As long as I have known Henry, I have never had a chance to see his romantic side.

He presents himself as always efficient and motivated for factual results. However, when I watch him with his family, I get a glimpse into this man's true heartbeat.

Before the snows forced us to return to the Head Office, I knew Henry was doubtful of what we had witnessed in the Southern Palliser and felt unsure about suggesting the land as suitable for sale through the Dominion Lands Act. Since our return, Henry and I have been reading the 1857 report by Captain John Palliser as well as the 1870 follow-up report by the Canadian biologist, John Macoun.

More in my next letter.

My most heartfelt loving New Year's wishes to all of you,

Albert

******

March 1, 1892

My Dear Family,

Henry and I have spent these last, long winter months back at Regina's Head Office transferring survey information onto homestead documents. As well, we have been occupied with extensive conversations, correspondence, and readings regarding Palliser's assessments of the land that I mentioned in a previous letter.

No administrators in Ottawa's Dominion Land Survey Bureau appeared ready to accept our suggestions that the Palliser Region homestead grants be suspended. We understand how radical a proposal this is, and believe me dear family, I would not be following Henry's lead in this regard if I did not feel it entirely worthy of consideration. Henry and I both know our very livelihoods (and reputations) are at stake. To oppose an entire government's authority for land acquisition is formidable.

Before the snows forced us to leave our surveying for the winter months, Henry and I abandoned our original mandate. We began to travel extensively throughout the Southern Palliser, trying to understand the government's position in licensing this desolate and uncultivable land to immigrant settlers.

Government sentiment, at the time the Canadian Pacific Railway was being built, was adamant that the forty-ninth parallel be protected. When the National Geographic Society underwrote Palliser's 1857 expedition, he reported back that he had entered "a kind of hell." He wrote there was nothing that recommended the Palliser as suitable for cultivation. The only area suitable was a fertile belt outside the Palliser surrounding the northern region, which he felt could be recommended. This more favourable assessment asserted that the fertile strip along the North Saskatchewan River Valley was larger than expected and had sufficient rainfall to sustain agriculture.

Confederation expansionists ignored Palliser's assessment and hired a Canadian agricultural botanist named Macoun who was to visit the area and write his own report. John Macoun's report bolstered hopes of the Palliser being suitable for cultivation. He concluded that it would become successful wheat land because rainfall occurred when it was needed. Macoun had provided the agricultural justification necessary for locating the CPR main line through these ill-suited prairie grasslands.

The possibility of such an assessment gladdened the expansionists. Although Palliser had submitted a report on the region's ill-suited conditions, the British government ignored it and encouraged settlement in the area, even as Mother Nature, with her recurrent droughts encouraged the opposite.

I will write further on this situation soon.

Love to all,

Albert

CHAPTER 7

PYOTR

The parcel we choose to cultivate first is along the river. We feel it is the most suitable but first we need to clear it of rocks and trees. The stand of trees that divide this parcel from the river we will leave in place. The trees will hold the soil and form an attractive barrier through which we will walk when going to the river.

Clearing the land of stumps and rocks is backbreaking work but Baba works alongside me daily with the end product of a new log house as our goal. At night we sit in our humble sod shack, drawing out the plans for our new log structure, which becomes more elaborate every day. We will locate our log house where we dig our well of course, so, first things first.

Digging a well is dangerous work. I remember as a small boy of hearing about the many catastrophes that could occur with cave-ins and drownings. Since I am splitting great stacks of wood for sale, I am able to barter winter wood in exchange for wells to be dug for our four families with a local farmer who is considered the area's best well digger. It is from him that I learn how useful it is for a farmer to have another trade. That seems to be how he started; by helping his neighbours and soon being considered a professional to be paid for his services.

With our plans coming along, my grandmother feels it was now time for me to attract a wife. She knows with the building of our new log house that a suitable wife will find a charming log home environment most inviting. We have the floor plan laid out for a large three-bedroom house, one of which will be Baba's bed and sitting room with its own outside entrance.

Baba tells me constantly that it's high time I was married. There are several young women of a suitable age in our area, one of whom is Jakob's sister, Julia. She seems drawn to me, but I don't feel a great attraction for her. Julia would be an excellent choice as a farmer's wife for the right farmer. She understands the difficulties and hardships of working the land. Mikhail and Ivan's wives are constantly telling me how good a match we would make. I know I have disappointed the families and especially Baba by not choosing Julia. My grandmother was so hoping Julia and I would come together but I'm afraid I could not love her as she deserves. In no way did I want to hurt her feelings, but I was finally forced to tell her I could only be her friend. What do I know of women? Everything is rushing at me too fast. Slow down, Pyotr, my Myushka says. Everything will play out as it should. Sound advice from a cat.

CHAPTER 8
MARY AND LIZZIE

I keep Lizzie occupied for most of her summer days before returning to school with filling special orders for my Active Modern clothing line. Tennis, cycling, badminton, day hiking, swimming, and rowing are becoming welcome alternatives to the accepted activities for most young women outside the drawing rooms of 1900s Toronto. The highly stacked Gibson Girl hairstyles are being replaced with more restrained versions incorporating braids and buns, worn low at the nape of the neck.

Corsets have been loosened considerably or completely discarded by the athletic set although the *doyens* of fashionable Toronto feel this scandalous act encourages rough, masculine behaviours. Lizzie and I know there are widespread social expectations for women, but it seems there is an increased demand for suitably modest clothing for riding bicycles or swinging a tennis racquet.

Lizzie and I field test all our own clothing designs. In doing a variety of vigorous athletic activities, we decide that almost the same level of physical exertion is needed by chambermaids, charwomen, scullery workers, and loom spinners. No wonder the upper-class women generally loathe to perspire. Perhaps it is too ordinary and common.

CHAPTER 9

ALBERT

May 10, 1903

Dear Family,

My birthday was made remarkably special with the arrival of your parcel filled with three beautifully framed family portraits. Your careful packaging protected all the glass and frames. It was most thoughtful to wrap the final bundle in one of your beautiful quilts Mother. The family group photo was made even more remarkable in that everyone looks so well. I was instantly smitten with little Albert hugging Old Brute who now appears so exceedingly aged that I can't believe he is still romping through the forests chasing rabbits. I can not count the many times he would rest one of his front paws on my foot as I sat in your office Father. Sister, your little cabbages have now turned into giant beanstalks. How beautiful they all are.

From my recent letters, you know how conflicted Henry and I have been over recommending the unsuitable land of the Palliser as good farmland for immigrant homesteaders. It is because of our travels through the Palliser Region that Henry and I felt, in all good conscience, we could not be affiliated with the Dominion Lands Commission any longer. So, to that end, the new offices of Kirkham and Goodfellow have been formed. Yes, Henry and I have left our government positions and struck out on our own. Together, we have formed a company and have new offices here in Regina! We have formed our own survey and land management company, which is proudly headquartered in Saskatchewan's capital.

This letter is going to be short because the next news I give you is really my biggest news. I will soon be standing in front of you. Yes, it's true. This coming holiday will be my first return home in many years and I'm bringing someone very special to meet my extraordinary family.

Henry Kirkham and I are now related not only through our company partnership but also through marriage, for I have become the proudest of husbands and his son-in-law! Abigail is Henry's older daughter and such a beauty she is. Family, I have never known such complete peace and joy. I realize you've had no knowledge of my intentions but rest easily with my decision. I have been accepted into a well-established and respected family who live in Saskatchewan's capital city. For now, Abigail and I have residence in the beautiful Kirkham house but will soon move to our own home, which will be situated near the province's ornate and impressive government legislature.

We will be arriving to meet you on April 1, on the 3:15 p.m. afternoon train. Our tickets are secured, and we are already packing our bags. My Abi has never been out of Saskatchewan and is excited to embrace my whole family in one gigantic hug. You will love her as I do.

Most affectionately,

Abigail and Albert

******

May 30, 1903

Dearest Family,

Following on the heels of our most memorable visit with you, Abigail and I have now safely returned to our home here in Regina. Henry and Amelia supervised the construction of our new house while we were with you. On our visit, did you specifically order that remarkable spring weather? Each and every one of you made Abigail feel instantly welcomed into the Goodfellow fold. You certainly made me a proud man.

We are now able to share our exciting new news with certainty. Abigail suspected she was possibly pregnant when we were with you but wanted to make sure before getting your hopes up. It was all I could do not to spill the beans on several occasions! I did whisper it to little Albie and ol' Brute one evening but an easily distracted seven-year-old and an ancient arthritic dog know how to keep a secret. So, yes, we are expecting our baby before Christmas. Can life be made any richer than what I feel here and now.

Abigail is out shopping with her mother at the moment but sends her love. Her health is good, and the doctor feels confident there will be no complications.

Much love,

Albert and Abigail

******

December 23, 1903

Darling Sister,

A separate letter has been sent to Father and Mother but, to you, most loving of sisters, I wanted to express my secret feelings about the birth of my two beautiful boys.

Abi's happy confinement was made all the sweeter by the early arrival of two of this world's more remarkable creations. Even our doctors were surprised as there was no indication of Abigail carrying two babies. Small Henry and Caleb (Father will be pleased!) were a week premature but have each arrived healthy and hungry. Although both were slightly jaundiced at birth, they have each responded well to the bili light so we were able to bring them home three days ago.

Abigail is waited on hand and foot by her whole family and seems to have readily taken to supplying ample nutrition. Thank heavens for Abi's family for I seem incapable of doing anything constructive. I gaze at great lengths into their cribs with red-rimmed eyes, slowly shaking my head at my wonderful good fortune.

I feel overwhelmed by such bounty and now feel the enormous weight of responsibility. At these times, I look into Abigail's eyes, and I see how she trusts me to be the best father I can be.

Your brother,

Albert

CHAPTER 10

PYOTR

The very first time Pyotr saw Miss Lizzie Dooley, she was standing beside her bicycle as he overtook her on the road into town. Pyotr was driving a wagon to a cattle market to purchase some new livestock. Lizzie had stopped to gaze across a large field of young wheat and seemed lost in the sweeping beauty of what lay before her. He saw her standing against the bright blue sky in her green dress with the wind gently pulling at several strands of stray hair. He thought those wisps were the exact colour of the wheat before her. For Pyotr it would be one of those indelibly etched moments in his memory. He was instantly captivated.

Taking little notice of the approaching wagon, Lizzie was suddenly startled from her reverie. She flashed a short smile in his direction before once more mounting her bicycle. Pyotr continued along the road and when he glanced back, he saw she had turned off onto a side path and was pedalling through the trees in the direction of the new schoolhouse. She would later tell him that yes, she did remember the encounter but had no distinct memory of him. It was the large grey and white cat sitting up on his shoulder that had impressed her.

Over the next few days, Pyotr found the image of this unknown woman was on his mind constantly. Discreet inquiries were not required because everyone was talking about the new schoolteacher's arrival along with her mother. As well, the whole township knew of the innocent mistake in the newspaper advertisement that had so captivated her.

CHAPTER 11

LIZZIE

My inspiration to become an educator I attribute solely to the influence of Miss Lucy Ambrose who shall ever represent the pinnacle of beauty, purpose, and elegance in my mind. No woman, other than my mother, has ever stood on such a pedestal. They are both completely unique.

After my high school graduation and one year of teachers' college in Toronto, I began to entertain the notion of leaving the big city and heading into Canada's interior. To begin my teaching career in such a newly established territory was very appealing. I had no difficulty persuading my mother of my exciting plan. She was always game for an adventure. We did, however, need to address the responsibilities of her tailoring business plus the three seamstresses she had hired to provide piecework.

If I moved to a new location, my mother, of course, would come with me.

Many of Mama's clients expressed opinions as to the foolishness of putting such an emphasis on a teaching career when, at my age, my sole purpose should be to secure a husband. Mama was very indulgent of those who put forth such opinions. We would chuckle and mock those women behind their backs when we were alone. My mother had developed a thriving fashion business quite outside of the mainstream dressmaking trade of Toronto and had built up a large clientele of very influential patrons. Her three hired seamstresses would be sad to lose her but were only too happy to receive their new sewing machines as a parting gift.

It was a newspaper article in the Canadian Agriculturist that had captured my attention. The opening of Canada's interior provinces presented exciting opportunities for many tradesmen (and women) outside of farming. Townships were being organized after the land was surveyed. Following the completion of the railway and the driving of the last spike, a wide range of businesspeople, Catholic nuns and priests, nurses, doctors, lawyers, mounted police, telephone operators, pharmacists, veterinarians, secretaries, salesmen, builders, retail merchants, and teachers were encouraged to move west.

The Three Sisters

My eye was caught by a particular advertisement that detailed the description of a newly constructed schoolhouse with a wide front porch plus an adjoining teacher accommodation (two bedrooms, kitchen, and sitting room with a fireplace). But what was so intriguing about this advertisement were the final words located below the description of the buildings stating, "a pony included." A pony! What more enticement would anyone need?

******

It was enthralling to travel away from Toronto, chugging along while gazing out the train's windows as we passed through the endless lake system of Ontario. It seemed to go on and on and on but finally we reached the massive rail yards in Winnipeg. I could not believe such an expanse of train tracks could exist. Our train is filled with families heading west, mostly homesteaders, but there are some regular working folks like us.

Three days later we arrived at our destination in Southern Saskatchewan where we transferred our goods to a spur line heading north. There, we were met by the mayor and his wife who helped us transport our boxes, bags, valises, and trunks onto two trucks to their township's newly designated school site.

"Welcome, Miss Dooley. You and your mother will be the first occupants of our new school and living quarters," began the mayor's wife. "And all the local farmers and town's people are so excited to meet you. We have fourteen students also ready to greet you when school starts in three weeks. We feel we're really on the map now with our very own professional teacher! And you'll love your school site. We've had a well dug and a raised rock wall built for safety with a bucket and rope in place. The outhouse has been dug, situated quite close to the school and newly painted. Some of the Christian Temperance Women from town have filled your larder with pies and stews and . . ."

"Is there a shed for the pony?" I interrupted.

"Pony? There's no shed for a pony, my dear. Also, there's no pony. We have built a paddock for the students' horses but no barn yet. We'll get that done before winter. Perhaps . . . if you purchase a . . . horse . . ."

I took out my well-worn advertisement from the newspaper as well as my letter of acceptance from the mayor's office.

"But your advertisement clearly states . . . pony included."

"Let me see that newspaper clipping," she said. "Oh, my dear, they've misspelled . . . there's been a mistake . . . I'm so sorry for the confusion. It's supposed to say phone not pony."

I didn't hear the rest although she continued to talk.

". . . very proud that the school is connected by the newly installed telephone system so you can reach the police constabulary, the local hospital, and the mayor's office. The switchboard is located in the basement of our town hall. Muriel Pearson is our telephone operator and will connect you to a few of the residents who have allowed telephone lines to reach their houses. Your ring at the school is three shorts. Any other questions?"

******

"They must all think I'm a complete fool, Mama. That story will soon spread. They will ridicule me forever."

"Nonsense. They're farmers and a farming community's people. They love animals and they'll love you because you love animals. It's actually a rather endearing mistake on your part. Feel absolutely no shame."

My mother was completely right. And on the very first day of school, fourteen students were enrolled, and each brought me a drawing, wooden carving, or poem about a pony. It was the sweetest gesture I could imagine. I felt like the whole township had embraced me.

The first time I saw Pyotr, he was astride a large brown stallion leading a smaller dappled beige and white mare, which was following behind. What was even more startling was the huge grey and white cat perched on his left shoulder. As they approached the schoolyard, the cat descended from his shoulder and wiggled its long body inside his shirt, which made a most curious bulge above his belt. My students had all been dismissed for the day and were milling about saddling their horses. Since many of them rode their own horses to school, the paddock allowed for the students' horses to be unsaddled until dismissal. They were delighted by this romantic display and exchanged many sly smiles and winks in my direction. My mother and I were sitting on the front porch of the teacherage having tea.

"I wanted to bring you a real pony," he said by way of introduction. "She's a little bigger than a pony but I think she will fit you nicely. My name is Pyotr. I am pleased to meet you and your mother. I live just down the river."

He descended from his horse and made a slight bow to us. It was so sweet and so unexpected. My mother immediately poured him a cup of tea.

"Pyotr, you need to know, I've never been on a horse."

"Then let's have tea followed by a short riding lesson. Since the sun is going down in a few hours, I suggest you try sitting in the saddle while I lead Sunny around your front yard. We will meet again, perhaps soon? And have another riding lesson. I will stable your horse on my homestead until you are comfortable stabling her here. I've named her Sunny . . . Sunshine. Don't you think that's a good name? I know you two will become great friends."

I quickly changed into one of Mama's split skirts and allowed Pyotr to show me how to mount from the left. He was right. I was instantly smitten with Sunny.

After that first meeting, Pyotr and I made a habit of daily riding lessons. There was no sense trying to keep any of this a secret. The romantic inclinations on Pyotr's part were easily seen every time he looked at me.

******

During my first prairie autumn, it was like the earth was alive and singing to me. I couldn't hear enough of the meadowlarks and the cicadas' buzz. Wheat fields held me captive and made a particular shushing noise in the breeze. All of what was spread before me was so alive. And in each of those many years before, as I had been seated at my childhood factory loom, these Saskatchewan prairie fields had existed, right here, in just this way. I had had no knowledge of any of this as my focus had been narrowed and stunted by the repetitive labour. It now seemed impossible that these two worlds had existed at the same time.

It was my students who told me of the early tribes of the Plains who had herded the stampeding buffalo off the cliffs just south of our little schoolhouse. They would bring me their collected arrowheads from that jump and many times they were still deeply embedded in the animal bones. Some of these arrowheads were fashioned from volcanic obsidian. How could that be possible? Early Cree had also mixed buffalo meat and berries to make pemmican, often used as a survival food during the harsh seasons. These round, hard, petrified, leather-covered caches were constantly being kicked up when the homesteads were plowed. How had my instincts known to find this wonderful land? How had this wonderful land, in turn, known to attract me.

Journal Entry

September 10, 1903

With each passing season, there is evidence of my unique position in this newly formed township. I now have two years invested in my teaching career and feel the rewards are many. I find great joy in teaching the children of homesteaders. This school year I am enrolling twenty students. Some are from town, but most are from nearby farms. Once again, I marvel at their good nature and curiosity for learning. I feel I have everything I want. My independent lifestyle may be questioned by many, but I delight in being able to support myself through such enjoyable work and answering to no one (except a rather demanding local school authority).

It is Mama who repeatedly makes mention of the fact that I need to be more aware and sensitive to the number of young men who desire my attention. Single women of marriageable age are highly sought. I know this; I am not being coy. Any farming community needs the stability of the pioneer and his wife, together, tilling the soil and enduring the harsh prairie seasons. But in my mind, I know I am definitely not interested in being a farmer's wife. I was indentured early in my life, and I have absolutely no interest in ever being shackled again. The demands of the land are onerous. Much as I love these prairies, I witness the continued hardships of turning the earth, planting the seed, and then praying for good weather. Or enough rain. I watch the young farming mothers of my students. They are old before their time. Their worries for successful crops are constant.

Journal Entry

August 29, 1904

Pyotr and I kissed! Or rather, he kissed me. I sensed he always wants to do this but is too shy. We were riding out yesterday and when we stopped to let the horses drink, he leaned toward me and kissed me on the side of my mouth. We were both still in the saddle and the moment was quite awkward. I was so surprised that I must have dug my heels into Sunny, and she suddenly bolted. I didn't handle the situation very well and started to laugh while trying to get my horse under control. Pyotr eventually started to laugh as well but he looked frustrated by his impulsive move. It was an odd sideways kiss and maybe not quite how he had planned it. I liked him kissing me a lot and told Mama when I returned home. She had a peculiar look on her face and may be worried I will experience the same outcome as what she endured at fifteen. We don't really ever talk about her attack in his Lordship's house.

It's odd for me to think of the man who violated my mother as my father. She shares everything with me, yet I don't even know what he looked like. Mama and I have always talked freely about the ways of men and women but suddenly we seem to have stopped. Maybe she's concerned when I'm alone with Pyotr.

Journal Entry

September 10, 1904

Another school year begins. Mama and I continue to feel such peace and contentment within this growing farm community. She has started a small dressmaking and tailoring business in one corner of our sitting room and finds new clientele walking through our door every week. I have happily given over this small space to her sewing needs although I can see she does seem to need more room. Between the activities in my schoolhouse and her new customers, our front yard is always busy with folks coming and going.

I'm also thinking a lot about how I feel when I'm with Pyotr. I know I'd like to touch him, and I think I'd like him to touch me. But he's so shy and it feels unnatural for me to take the lead.

Journal Entry

October 12, 1905

Pyotr and I continue to ride together when he is able to leave his farm chores. It's often far more peaceful to saddle up Sunny and head out on my own. He suggested I teach him to read in exchange for riding instructions but his interest wanes quickly, which is disappointing to me. I think it's just a ploy on his part to spend more time sitting close together.

I see Pyotr's lovesick gaze and I feel such guilt knowing I can't return his same feelings. I do love him, and I know he wants to be physically closer. I'm afraid if I let him kiss me, he will think I want him to touch me, which I do when I feel a wave of longing. But then I hear my mother's voice.

Yes, I do love him but not enough to enter into marriage. He is a wonderful man; no one needs to sing his praises to me. Pyotr is a true farmer, and he needs a woman who would be a dedicated farmer's wife. Pyotr is probably everything I would ever want but I know in my heart I could not be his kind of farm wife. I would be required to leave my little schoolhouse and my students if I married. I would then be literally chained to the stove and the farm's domestic demands. As much as I think I love him, I know I would soon resent him. Why would I want to marry an illiterate farmer?

Journal Entry

October 13, 1905

Mean, spiteful words. He has shown me nothing but kindness.

Journal Entry

November 1, 1906

Recently, I sensed Pyotr's friendship with me has taken a serious turn for the worse. I know I have no one to blame for this dilemma but myself. I have not been completely forthright with him.

Yesterday, after school, we rode out along the river. It was chilly and the oncoming winter was in the air. He said his harvesting duties were complete and he had no pressing farm demands. I truly was not aware of his intentions on that particular late afternoon. We tethered our horses and walked through the trees to his homestead site where his grandmother was peeling bark from cut logs for their future house.

He turned suddenly and once again declared his love for me. He said he wanted us to be married. He felt he had waited long enough and needed an answer. I showed great hesitancy and an unsmiling face in considering this declaration. Many long seconds passed in which I simply stared at him and said nothing.

It seems I have now wounded his pride so deeply that I despair. My intention was never to cause either of us such grief, but I see that is what has happened. I have been a coward in allowing him to think there was the possibility of a great love between us. Friendship, yes. A deeper love? I'm not sure. I know it's more than a friendship. I know it as I write these words. I'm sure that's how I feel.

Journal Entry

September 5, 1908

The start of another school year. I am again enrolling twenty students this September, many of whom are the younger siblings of children I have taught in the past. I guess I'm now considered "the old maid schoolteacher" by the community. I am fine with that although after attending a recent rash of summer weddings, I do feel a bit melancholy today. One of those wedding celebrations was for Pyotr, which occurred (thankfully) in another community. I would have felt many complex emotions if I had attended his ceremony. I do know that I want only good things for him and wish him every happiness. But still, I feel such a loss in my life.

My mother senses my continued turmoil but says nothing. Bless her.

Journal Entry

April 12, 1909

I experience the same overwhelming delight with the approach of every new season but prairie springtime is probably my favourite. We planted crocus beds around the schoolhouse and they are suddenly starting to come into bloom . . . a sure sign of spring. I hear the robins during the day, which always feels like a sign. Even the air smells differently. Wheat fields have been under a thick winter snow blanket and are readying themselves to receive the seed. I feel such contentment when I gaze at these beautiful prairie fields.

I rarely see Pyotr anymore. I know he has just become a new father. His wife has given birth to a little girl. They've named her Eva. When I heard this news, I felt both happy and sad.

He and his grandmother have finished their new log house and I am told it's beautiful. I know he is kept busy with his little family. It is unreasonable of me to still expect his attention. Our visits by horseback cannot happen as they used to, and I miss them so much. I keep Sunny stabled here at the school and she continues to appear strong and healthy. The local veterinarian seems pleased with her health and how often she is being exercised. There is no need to involve Pyotr with her care.

I wonder if his wife knows about me.

Journal Entry

August 10, 1914

This afternoon, Mama and I watched the enlisted men of our small-town board the train to begin their journey to Europe. It confounds me how eager they are to sacrifice themselves for a war that doesn't involve Canada. They are all proudly wearing newly issued Canadian uniforms and looking so hopeful, anticipating their big war adventure. Past the many heads of the send-off crowd, I could see Pyotr with his wife and grandmother standing away from the main group. His grandmother returned my gaze with a stern scowl. I have always known she felt my rejection of Pyotr's proposal propelled him into marrying someone else. I am sorry it has come to this, even after all these years. As they turned to leave, I could see Pyotr's wife in profile. He will soon become a father again.

His little Eva is doing so well in my Grade 1 class. I confess to feeling a great partiality in seeing her sweet, freckled face every morning. She always calls me "Miss Lizzie" and now the other students have followed suit. I enjoy seeing Pyotr every afternoon when he comes to pick her up, but we rarely have eye contact. Pyotr's wife, Natalia is also very sweet but rarely speaks with me, allowing Pyotr to answer for her. Apparently, Pyotr met her through the large Jewish farming community called Edenbridge, which established a settlement in the eastern section of our province. She is a beautiful young woman and I think she will give Pyotr the large family he wants.

My daily life and the life of my enterprising mother (who now fashions hats!) continues along at an even pace despite the intrusion of this horrid war. As Mama and I watched our boys' departure, I happened to take note of a flamboyant group of very fancy women who stepped off the train at the same time as we waved farewell to our departing group of soldiers. These flashy women appeared to be accompanied by a dapper gentleman wearing very big city clothes.

Journal Entry

September 15, 1916

This morning four members of the stringently minded Women's Christian Temperance Union made a visit to my small country schoolhouse to ensure that my teachings are in accordance with their adherence to scripture. They appear to have a strong need to impose teetotalling views on every aspect of our little township and seem overly single-minded in their rigid approach to everyday life. I agree with Mama, that the excesses of alcohol can erode the work ethic on which this province's settlement depends, but how is it that any thinking adult should adhere to such authoritarian demands? It only raises the attraction of breaking the very rules the Women's Christian Temperance Union seeks to establish.

******

The Three Sisters

"And what gives this organization the right to oversee our morality?" I ask my mother as we sit down for tea at the end of the day. School had been dismissed. I was still fuming over the demands made by this delegation of self-righteous women to ensure my teachings met their moral standards.

"I cover all the recommended subject areas. I address the requirements for reading, writing, and mathematics for all my students. I keep them interested with lessons in geography and immigrant origins. We study the Indigenous people of this region as well as the local plant and animal life. This year I have organized constructive activities for twenty students who range in age from six to seventeen. We host a Christmas concert and an event in the spring. And **now**, these busybody women feel I need to preach the evils of alcohol and how liquor is responsible for domestic violence. **And** poverty. **And** the degradation of society?"

"Calm yourself, Lizzie. The WCTU existed long before the threat from the newly arrived Mr. Bigelow and his questionable coterie of female companions. Hopefully, these guardians of our morality with their prohibition on liquor will soon realize their strict adherence to propriety is better delivered through the church. That's where their message really should originate."

******

It was several days later when Mr. Bigelow himself drove a wagon containing five giggling women into our schoolyard and stopped in front of our little house. I left the children to complete their assigned schoolwork and crossed the yard to our front porch. I could see my mother engaged in conversation with Mr. Bigelow.

"Mother, what is this all about?" I inquire.

"Well, it seems Mr. Bigelow is seeking a dressmaker."

She turned to our visitors and said, "Mr. Bigelow. Ladies. This is my daughter, Miss Lizzie Dooley."

"What a pleasure it is to meet you both," he replied smoothly, removing his cigar as he spoke.

Turning back to my mother, he said, "Mrs. Dooley, I made inquiries in town at the general store and was given your name as a skilled dressmaker. I was hoping you could take the necessary measurements for my five lovely hostesses and provide each with a new dress."

After they all followed Mama into our house, I returned to supervise my students. I knew my mother and I would be discussing this further after I dismissed school for the day.

******

"Mama," I began, "don't you realize how difficult this will be for me? If my recent visit from the Christian Temperance Women is any indication of their concerns for our community's morality, your involvement with Mr. Bigelow and his hostesses will seriously compromise me."

"I know I put our positions at risk, Lizzie. But I could hardly turn them away. I had absolutely no idea he would arrive here with his ladies . . . and, in the back of a wagon, like so many sacks of bran, for heaven's sake! I felt it would be rude not to invite them in and at least consider his business proposal. And, Lizzie, he is willing to pay handsomely . . . for five dresses!"

I had to agree with my mother. As much as I loved my job, I felt an overwhelming temptation to thumb my nose at the Women's Christian Temperance Union with their holier-than-thou attitudes and demands. Word did spread quickly about Mr. Bigelow and his fancy ladies visit to our home. When the community heard of my mother offering her dressmaking skills to his hostesses, there was an undercurrent of outrage from the expected sources.

Two weeks later, Mama and I arranged for a neighbour to help us deliver her beautifully sewn new dresses to Mr. Bigelow. He had established himself and his five ladies in the three side by side houses quite removed from town. These houses had been originally built for three members of a farming family who had been unable to take ownership for unknown reasons. Sitting empty, they had been advertised for sale across Canada in several newspapers. These three houses now provided the perfect opportunity for a carpetbagger like Mr. Thaddeus Bigelow to take ownership. His plan had always been to create a bootleg alcohol and gambling venue outside the limits of a prairie township. He had secured an illegal liquor supply from a source in North Dakota that would be regularly trucked across the border into Southern Saskatchewan under the cover of darkness.

******

Apparently, the rows and rows of the many cars, horses, and wagons outside The Three Sisters on a Saturday night is downright scandalous, as the WCTU women continue to inform me. On their next visit, they requested my mother and I become part of their brigade and help in listing the names of those men who would frequent such an establishment. I am in no way a supporter of public shaming. I now fear my teaching contract may be in jeopardy. I do love teaching the children of these stalwart prairie settlers and feel my mother and I are an integral part of this community. However, I am beginning to realize we may have to leave Saskatchewan. Until prohibition is lifted, we will encounter the same wrong-headed thinking everywhere in this province. So, when my contract ends in June, Mama and I are thinking we may have to travel even farther west.

"Women everywhere always like pretty hats and dresses," she chirps. "We're resilient. We'll survive."

******

Journal Entry

June 30, 1916

It is with great sadness that Mama and I now leave the southern prairies. The Women's Christian Temperance Union has influenced the school board in demanding my resignation. I have not a single argument left with which to present my case before these officials. They have even accused me of foregoing marriage, which they feel would have assured my compliance.

I have such an intense connection to my little country schoolhouse, my first teaching location, and the many children I have instructed. It is extremely special to me.

Mama and I stood on the railway platform experiencing an odd mixture of remorse and a great sense of adventure. I write this journal entry now as we make our way west toward the mountain community of Banff. I am not assured of any kind of teaching position, but I feel a sense of general optimism. We will arrive soon at the mountains! I imagine we will gaze out the windows of our club car at vistas we have only seen on CPR posters and magazines.

I understand the township's desire for support of the Temperance Union's ideals of prohibition but find it impossible in my heart to agree with such rigid values. I leave behind my many wonderful students who over the past years have given back to me the richness of their immigrant cultures. I leave behind my darling Sunny, which Pyotr has graciously taken back onto his farm for stabling. Sadly, he asked a neighbour to come by for the horse, so I was unable to say a personal goodbye.

It seems Pyotr was recently cited as a found-in (among many others) in the latest WCTU scandal that listed patrons visiting The Three Sisters. I think Pyotr's involvement, however minor, added to his sadness after the unexpected death of his beloved grandmother. Perhaps this confirms the persistent rumour about Pyotr and one of Thaddeus Bigelow's hostesses, a woman named Rosie. This troubles me slightly but I have no way of knowing if it's true. Apparently, Rosie's additional skills as a midwife have become widely sought since her arrival and she is often called upon in troublesome births. It is rumoured that Pyotr formed an attachment to her at the time of his second daughter's difficult birth and now makes frequent visits to the "Sisters".

It seems unnecessary to punish these farmers for taking a drink or two when it is they who are responsible for supplying the world's pantries with grain during this endless war.

As of last week, the Temperance Union and their prohibition mandate have brought about the closing down of those notorious Three Sisters houses and they now stand empty once again. I was told one of the houses was used for fine dining. It had velvet drapes and was decorated with an elegant style of imported wallpaper. The other two houses provided liquor for patrons and various forms of gambling. It was widely known that Bigelow's hostesses used the rooms upstairs for their own questionable purposes. Bigelow had even imported a casino roulette wheel all the way from San Francisco!

Apparently, a few mornings ago, Bigelow and his ladies were unceremoniously turned out of their three houses without any warning. We heard it was quite a sight witnessing their sudden forced exodus. The men and women of the WCTU certainly exacted their pound of flesh. The townsfolk crowded the streets leading to our train station to watch as Bigelow and his fancy hostesses were forced to take the noon train. People actually cheered as it pulled away.

Mama and I made a point of visiting Pyotr's grandmother's gravesite before our own departure. We could see several small pebbles had been left on top of her marker.

Her headstone read:

Here lies Sonia Sophia Maria Kowalluk

1840–1916

She was a hard worker

It sounds like such an unsentimental description for such a wonderful woman, but in Pyotr's eyes there could be no greater tribute. His grandmother resolutely stood by his side through every challenge. When feeling fatigued from one farm task, she would rest by undertaking another.

CHAPTER 12

NEW RECRUIT ALBERT GOODFELLOW

August 15, 1916

My Dearest Father and Sister,

I write this letter to properly explain my lengthy deliberation regarding my enlistment in Canada's wartime participation. This will probably be the last letter you will receive before I am deployed to France. My enlistment is almost complete, and I am to be made a proud foot soldier in the Canadian effort supporting our British interests overseas. I know that Abigail and our twin boys will be well looked after when I am away contributing my services to Britain's involvement in Europe's war.

I realize Henry, Amelia, and Abigail are most displeased with my decision and question my allegiance to Britain in a war that is so far away. They see my involvement in the affairs of the British Empire as pure folly, but I see it as part of my heritage. Just as my great, great, great grandfather demonstrated his loyalty to King George during America's Revolutionary War, I obey the rule, "Where Britain leads, Canada will follow." We were told last year this war would be over by Christmas. It was promised to be a quick victory, but I fear it drags on. I want to do my part.

Your loving son,

Albert

******

Journal Entry

Albert Goodfellow, September 30, 1916

The festive air of excitement on the faces of the departing soldiers is not what I see reflected in Abigail's eyes. I can tell she is willing herself to appear composed. Henry and Amelia, her parents, have begged off saying goodbye at the station because of their upset and disapproval with my decision to enlist.

Henry's final words had been, "Albert, you'll be lucky not to be blown to bits. You're a right arse, you know that don't you!"

Only Abigail and our twin boys were with me on the platform. I am so sorry to think of the time I will be missing with Caleb and Small Henry but continue to feel driven to contribute what I am able. I know I arrive late to this war effort but feel, after basic training, I will be able to add my effort. I am immensely heartened by the show of support from our immediate community. I will never, ever, forget their hopeful good wishes as all of us foot soldiers lined up, two deep, in blowing snow, outside Regina's Feed and Grain store before boarding the train to our training camp in Borden, Ontario. Camp Borden's construction has been hastily undertaken to meet the strenuous demands of Canada's military involvement. We'll soon begin our voyage to Europe to fight the oppression of the German and Austrian forces.

Journal Entry

Camp Borden, October 5, 1916, New Recruit A. J. Goodfellow

Our arrival by train, here in the newly created Camp Borden, is inauspicious. The camp numbers about 30,000 recruits, all preparing for deployment overseas. Prime Minister Borden's call to arms has been answered in record enlistments. On the train, I was surrounded by such young boys that I fear the enlistment regulations are being seriously breached. Some of my fellow recruits are only a few years older than my two young sweet boys. This thought makes me shudder.

I reminded myself that I am just a part of the great new recruit masses until, unexpectedly, I was singled out as potential leadership material. How has this happened, I know not. I sense this may be some of Henry's doing. Or perhaps, my father's. When I presented myself to my superiors, it was an informal interview. I am slow to consider my responses and carefully measure what I say. Perhaps this impresses my superiors. I can only say, I harken back to the advice from Father and my wonderful sister's constant harangue regarding eye contact and the reassuring smile needed to inspire confidence in my audience. It seems I'm regarded as a gentleman, which I guess is a good thing. I am told if my basic training proceeds well, I will be promoted to a leadership rank when we deploy to the European Front. This war has fast tracked the command hierarchy, it seems.

Daily, we are required to attend lectures regarding our geographic positions at the

Front. Canadian troops are being deployed to two fronts. The Western Front, the main theatre, is between France and Belgium and is called Vimy Ridge. And the Eastern Front is between Russia and Romania. Following the outbreak of war in August 1914, the German Army broke through the Western Front by invading Luxembourg and Belgium, thereby gaining military control of the important industrial regions in France.

Along Vimy Ridge, there is a new strategy of fighting called trench warfare. Hundreds of miles of trenches have been dug by both sides along this line. Now, armed with our newly issued Ross rifles, a replacement for the substandard Lee-Enfield, plus a new invention called the machine gun, we will volley shots at each other across an area called no man's land.

At Camp Borden, Canada has erected twenty-one miles of trenching to prepare new recruits. It's important to know how to live and work in such confined spaces. I can only imagine the added hardship of slogging through trenches filled with mud and water. Holding a line of defence with our bayonetted rifles, machine gun nests, grenades, and tank units is our only job. We are being asked to push the line as far back as possible until the enemy either retreats or surrenders. I am now told I will soon be deployed to the Western Front, to a place called Passchendaele, which is a destroyed village near Ypres in Belgium. This is a change in deployment, but it matters not. I'm anxious to do my part.

******

October 20, 1916

My Dearest Abigail, Caleb, and Small Henry, Amelia, and Big Henry,

My arrival at Camp Borden has gone smoothly and we have settled into military routines quickly. We are told our deployment to Europe will occur within the next month. I am housed along with sixty other new recruits in a building containing thirty bunk beds. Our days are spent in training and understanding the demands of trench warfare, learning Morse code, and artillery practice.

I have been singled out as a potential leader, probably more out of recognition of my maturity (age) than any innate ability for command. As the days have passed, I realize to properly lead a group of men that I need to know where I am going. This sobers me considerably. I know I would feel more comfortable as a non-commissioned officer. I'm not here for officer ranking. I've done nothing to earn that accolade. A regular foot soldier, I am.

I've pinned your drawings, Caleb and Small Henry, onto the wall at the head of my upper bunk. The young recruit (Ewan Williamson) who occupies the bed below me is quite taken with the artistry of my two young "scoundrels." He likes me to tell him stories of my life, which I have come to realize is quite remarkable. As seen through someone else's eyes, I guess it is. Ewen also has a stutter so I'm helping him learn to cope with it. He tells me of his interest in learning Morse code is quite ironic as communication has been a major problem all his life.

Soon, it will be lights out and I need to get this into an envelope to catch tomorrow's mail.

All my affection to you, Family. You know how very much I love you.

Albert

******

Journal Entry

January 1, 1917, Private Albert Goodfellow

We are a strong Canadian Contingent, CEF on our two-week Atlantic convoy ships' crossing. We sail in a massive fleet of ten troopships plus escorts toward Plymouth after which we will board trains for the

Salisbury Plains to the south. My placement remains the same: Passchendaele, a town in Belgium near Ypres on the Western Front. The British Crown has appointed a successor to Lieutenant-General E.A.H. Alderson who guided the Canadians well through the first two years of war, but these new appointments have caused unrest from the politicians of Ottawa. It seems the British feel there is inadequate Canadian leadership available.

******

Journal Entry

January 25, 1917, Albert Goodfellow

We follow in the footsteps of the many brave Canadian soldiers who have preceded us. One story we hear is of a battalion of 750 Newfoundlanders, all from one region of their island, wiped out completely in a single day at the battle of Beaumont-Hamel. Their sacrifice saddens me deeply.

It's stories like this that have given me the incentive to enlist.

We have begun our "cold and wet" training here in Salisbury. This is apparently one of Britain's coldest and wettest seasons in decades. Although we have stood up well, our original boots (British made) have not and have been discarded in favour of using stouter British replacement models. It's surprising to see the soles of such sturdy boots literally rot away so quickly.

This mobilization is hasty but for a group of young, wet-behind-the-ears prairie boys we've withstood the cold and discomfort extremely well. But I think we're all realizing our real training will start at the Front.

******

February 20, 1917

My Wonderful Wife and Family,

This will probably be my last letter for a while as we're shipping out to the Western Front tomorrow at dawn. Your heartwarming avalanche of letters needs to be tightly bound to fit into my rucksack. I can't bear to part with a single one and reread them constantly.

Caleb and Small, your fine drawings of the prairie landscapes and airplanes grace whatever cramped sleeping arrangement I'm allotted. I can see the two of you, sharing your crayons and pencils, heads bent over your masterpieces with intense focus.

Abigail, your photos are next to my heart.

Your loving Albert

******

Journal Entry

April 10, 1917, NCO Albert Goodfellow CEF

We are waiting in our trench position, here in Belgium in the countryside. We are near the bombed-out remains of a small village, quietly positioned as we were upon our arrival two days ago. It's past midnight and I'm on night watch. I look about me at the sleeping faces of men slouched in rude and uncomfortable positions; their helmets askew, mouths agape, and their gentle snoring cutting the stillness. I'm aware of the fierce need by our side to hold this line. We, of the infantry, need to hold this line. We need to protect this Allied land as "ours." I look out on a battlefield of water-filled craters and shell holes. I harken back to my first days with Henry, surveying the endlessly flat Saskatchewan landscape, staking long homestead pegs into the ground to establish ownership. There's a strange parallel behaviour here, this incessant fight to claim territory.

My uniform, issued when we left Saskatchewan, has been my one and only kit for the duration of our time in Britain and now here in the trenches near the Belgian border. Thank heavens I have new boots and a change of underwear and socks. But how I would love a hot bath. I'm told trench foot will soon settle in, and I'll be driven mad with the itching. Much advice is passed between the men as we wait. Infantry soldiers from the First Battle of Ypres tell the smokers to avoid "three on a match." I'm not a smoker but still, it's horrifying to think a German sniper needs only that length of time to take aim. I have also heard from the veterans that you never hear the bomb that has your name on it. The whistling sounds of bombs falling means they are falling far, far away. I'm not sure if that's meant to provide comfort but I appreciate the insight.

My young friend, Ewan Williamson, has confessed to me his real age is fifteen. This was revealed after a night terror, which reduced him to tears. I held him while he shook with grief in realizing he had left his widowed mother on her own in Saskatchewan to travel halfway across the world to fight a battle that might leave her grieving her only son's death.

He is overcome with guilt in abandoning his mother for what he thought would be a grand adventure. He says he awakens in the night seeing an image of her sitting alone at her kitchen table, weeping, with no one to offer comfort.

I can't write any of this to my family back home. I hope my journaled words will be read by someone who will understand the immense strain of waiting for an enemy encounter. I picture young Austrian and German boys, not five hundred yards away across no man's land, sitting in their water-filled muddy trenches, anticipating a similar fate.

******

May 25, 1917

To the Saskatchewan family of Albert Goodfellow, Canadian Infantry Prairie Division 70,

I am Nurse Nel Forsythe, RN, writing to you from the British Veterans Convalescent Hospital, Bristol, Ward 10, on behalf of NCO Albert Goodfellow

Dearest Family,

First of all, Albert is safe. He is alive and safe and is convalescing in hospital, on the cleanest of white linens. This seems to be of paramount importance to him that you know the conditions here are hygienic and highly antiseptic. He makes our nursing staff laugh with his great attention to our health protocols, "Has that instrument been sterilized?" "Do my dressings need to be changed?" "Should those windows be left open?" I assure you, he says this with the greatest respect for our professional opinions.

Albert has lost his left arm below the elbow but is determined to minimize this loss with, "it's not my dominant arm, so I guess I'm lucky!" And very fortunately, his temporary loss of vision has been fully restored because of hourly saline washes. Albert's right wrist is in a cast because it was also injured but will be fully restored in about two months. Since both arms are out of commission, Albert needs one of the nursing staff to maintain correspondence with his family.

Albert's unit was involved in the Third Battle of Ypres. The newspapers also refer to it as The Battle of Passchendaele, the tragic scene of a great loss of Canadian soldiers.

His battalion was subjected to a mustard gas attack, which is one of Germany's deadly concoctions. Albert and his men had been issued masks and protective gear. But on the afternoon in question, the bombs carrying the colourless gas began to readily infiltrate their trenches before they had masked up. It caused many of our men to also suffer loss of sight until their masks were in place. Perhaps Albert may have been slow to mask up or his mask may have been knocked out of a secure position when the poisonous shell containing the gas hit, but the explosion pinned him under rubble crushing his left arm and breaking his right wrist. Oddly, the Germans sound an audible gas gong for their own soldiers, so they know to mask up themselves in case of a sudden wind shift. When Albert is further healed, he will write at great length.

Yours sincerely,

Nurse Forsythe

******

July 28, 1917

To the wife and family of Albert Goodfellow,

From the hand of Milicent Smith-Shaw, RN, Bristol Convalescent Hsp., Ward 10

Dear Family,

Albert spends a large part of each day visiting the bedsides of his fellow Saskatchewan comrades. His young friend, Corporal

Williamson, acts as his wheelchair navigator to propel him through our corridors. Their corridor races have proven greatly beneficial in restoring morale as you can imagine, despite their more harrowing crashes, which leaves them all in a great heap. The medical staff has had to put a stop to these more destructive activities, which only makes them search out nighttime opportunities. It seems the British soon realized the benefits of keeping the Canadian troops together, rather than parcelling them out amongst other units. This policy has also been largely followed for those in convalescence as well. The men appear to have developed a great sense of unity.

Albert's good right arm is still in a cast so he is unable to write at present but wants you to know his wrist is healing well and will be soon fully functional. He says his missing left arm is bothering him slightly with phantom tingling but is minor compared to the lingering devastation endured by many in his company.

Germany had been unable to break through the Allied line at their location for three years. They were held off at great cost to our soldiers until they released their deadly form of gas bombs onto the Allied trenches at Passchendaele. Albert and his fellow soldiers were besieged for twelve straight hours by enemy aerial bombardment. One direct blast buried Albert for a full day under debris. He attributes his life to a combination of dumb luck despite his poorly positioned mask that allowed him to breathe until he could be dug out. A whole section of his trench had been obliterated. Apparently, the mustard gas even seeps into the mud and remains toxic in the trenches for days. Young Corporal Ewan Williamson worked tirelessly to free Albert and many others despite himself receiving a serious head wound and the loss of one eye. He has been recommended for valiant service.

Sincerely,

Nurse Smith-Shaw for Albert Goodfellow

******

September 30, 1917

To my most Darling Wife and Family,

Finally, my good right arm is out of its cast, and I can write my own words. At last! My vision has returned as well, and my eyes are clear. What a privilege to still be alive and tell, you, whom I hold most dear, how very much I love you. I find my joy in still being alive as something hard to express. This convalescent hospital is filled with soldiers who are not as fortunate as I. It is all around me every day. My feelings about religion have been thoroughly examined and I'm now in a position to know with great certainty that I have a guardian angel who has protected me through this hell.

The afternoon when our Canadian unit suffered its attack, it came after a three-year effort by the Germans to break the line here in Belgium. Our battalion had originally been ordered to another position along the Western Front, but new orders were received to remain in place.

When the poisonous shells containing the gas hit our section of the line, it was mayhem as we masked up and stood our position. At this point I wish I had a more heroic story to tell you. I don't remember much until I was dug out of the trench and triaged to a field hospital by several Red Cross soldiers. Those of us on stretchers were completely mud-caked, which made us unrecognizable to each other. All I could hear above the groans and cries was young Ewan calling out to me from somewhere in our field ambulance.

"You okay, Albert? You okay? Albert, speak to me!"

******

October 14, 1917

My Dearest Abigail,

In a few short days, I will be leaving the hospital here in England in the company of other discharged soldiers. I am with many wonderful men from my unit whom I've come to know well. Some are still on crutches; some still have visibly bandaged head or hand wounds. I am so fortunate to have escaped with only one coat sleeve pinned up to the elbow and the other in a sling. The break in my right arm has healed but I find the sling helps when my arm needs support.

Despite the excitement of returning to Canada, we are mainly a sombre bunch. Our time defending the line was short, but we feel our contribution was no less than the men who still remain. Although successfully holding the line at Passchendaele, the futility of lost lives is argued over feverishly by our Canadian politicians. It was their decision to send men to Europe in support of the Allies. They must share the responsibility for so many deaths on the battlefields.

I count the days until my train arrives at Regina's station and I can embrace my loved ones.

All my love to you,

Your Albert

******

December 20, 1917

To my dear Father and Mother-In-Law, Sister, Brother-in-law, and lovable Nieces and Nephews,

As I write this letter, I can see Albert sitting out on our back porch wrapped up in blankets and warm clothes. The air is very chilly, but he says he can hardly bear being indoors and needs to be outside no matter the weather. He is in his usual old wooden rocker with Caleb and Small Henry happily climbing all over him. They are really too big for these crazy antics, but Albert doesn't want to stop them from all their roughhousing. In the year and a half since Albert enlisted, the boys have had a remarkable growth spurt and I'm concerned they'll be too rough with him now that they are almost as tall as their father.

Albert has been home with us now for over a month and his convalescence is going well. He tells me the loss of his left arm is easy to endure and I'm not to fret unduly. The men in his unit suffered greater hardships he says, and many still suffer the effects of their mustard and phosgene gas attacks. I am kept busy maintaining correspondence with many of the soldiers in his unit. He seems to have been much loved, which gladdens my heart considerably and I know makes you feel proud of the man you know him to be.

We are so grateful to the British Red Cross units who assisted in his recovery. His many weeks spent in their hospitals were a great gift and led to his remarkable recuperation. I am most fortunate to have had my brave husband returned to me in (almost) one piece. This Christmas celebration will be exceptional for all of us.

Albert sends his warmest of (one armed) embraces and wants you to know he will soon be back to work with my father. Regina continues to expand, and its urban sprawl demands the continuing reliable services of Kirkham and Goodfellow. Albert's office is taking on a new apprentice urban surveyor, Ewan Williamson. Ewan was with him during the Third Battle of Ypres, at Passchendaele. Albert tells me Ewan is responsible, almost single-handedly, for his rescue so my gratitude is hard to control. It seems we now have a third son with whom Caleb and Small have formed a remarkable friendship. Ewan constantly complains that we have got to stop hugging him.

Your loving daughter-in-law and grandsons,

Abigail

Small Henry and Caleb send their bear hugs.

(Big) Henry and Amelia also send their regards.

CHAPTER 13
MARY AND LIZZIE

As our train pulls away from the station and we start our journey heading further west, I watch Lizzie's face as she fights back the tears. She breaks my heart, she does. I know her tears are partly out of frustration with the rigid policies enforced by the Women's Christian Temperance Union but also for the loss of her life with Pyotr. I want to yell at her for her resistance to marriage and making him suffer. But it is clear she also suffers in equal measure.

Our departure, unlike that of Thaddeus Bigelow along with his hostesses, is regarded as a great loss for our little farming community. Lizzie was much loved and respected. Her students, current and past, have gathered repeatedly to express disappointment for the decision to end her teaching contract. She will be sorely missed.

Tomorrow afternoon our train will arrive in Banff. Lizzie and I have read as much as we can find about what to expect when we step into our new life. Alberta's mountains are a far cry from the Saskatchewan prairies and an even farther cry from Liverpool. Never did I ever expect to see so much of Canada when we first stepped ashore in Quebec City so long ago.

LIZZIE

Journal Entry

July 15, 1916

Nothing has prepared us for the remarkable beauty of Banff. Mama and I stepped down from our train into one of the most picturesque little townsites we have ever seen. The air is so crisp and the skies so remarkably blue. All the National Park posters and brochures failed to match the feeling of standing in the midst of these mountains. We are constantly overwhelmed.

The impressive hotels connected to this cross Canada rail system look just like castles to me. We are told they are advertised worldwide and attract travellers, outdoorsmen, and mountaineers during every season.

With our several pieces of luggage and the assistance of a taxi service, Mama and I checked into a sweet little hotel, which also serves breakfast. It's quite a jolly place and filled with train travellers like us as well as a gregarious group of mountain climbers. We met them in the breakfast room on our first morning. They are a robust group, these energetic, suntanned French Canadians, who apparently have travelled across Canada to challenge themselves with strenuous hiking and canoeing. I am mindful of the difference between these mountaineers (who tell me they refuse to be part of Canada's wartime involvement) and all the men we know who have gone off to fight. Europe's battles now seem so far away as we sit here amid this scenery. Mama and I do take note of how few men there are in Banff despite these four mountaineers. We are told about forty young recruits left Alberta a few days ago heading for Camp Borden in Ontario. Politicians have had it hastily built to prepare the Canadian recruits.

Journal Entry

July 17, 1916

This morning, I watched my mother closely observing the rugged outdoor apparel of our mountaineers and I can tell her interest in designing suitably rugged clothing for women is returning. One morning at breakfast, she actually had the nerve to ask one of the men to remove his boots so she could examine them! I know she is visualizing this boot with the same low, sturdy heel suitable for a woman's foot. He seemed completely charmed to stand in his socks while Mama closely inspected his hiking boots. Pretty hats, indeed!

I remember many times seeing the wives of Saskatchewan farmers wearing their husband's rough clothing while working the fields or tending their animals. That kind of practicality seems completely lost on the active woman of our modern Edwardian era. I agree with my mother that women are starting to venture into rough wilderness activities like hiking over rough terrain or

Nordic skiing. The clothing available for these pursuits are fussy and cumbersome. Imagine, layers of petticoats still being worn under heavy tweed skirts while day hiking! Such nonsense.

Journal Entry

July 20, 1916

Mama and I spend every morning after breakfast walking the main streets of Banff. There is a unique architectural style to their buildings, which contributes to its mountain culture. It seems all construction projects need to be approved by the elected officials. What a conscientious mindset. I've never encountered such an idea in town planning.

We are not surprised that prohibition laws continue to be enforced throughout Alberta, much like what we encountered in Saskatchewan. The laws imposed by the government and reinforced by the Women's Christian Temperance Union are alive and well here! Hoorah for their team! But it appears, here in Banff, there is less appetite for such stringent regulations. I think people are simply bored and tired of this endless political argument.

Journal Entry

July 25, 1916

One morning on one of our walks, Mama saw an advertisement for a dressmaker's assistant in the window of a private residence. I swear, she practically turned a cartwheel! She kicked up her heels and we danced such a happy jig right there on the street. This is a remarkable opportunity for her. She does seem to know how to make her own good luck and keeps telling me, "It's a sign, Lizzie! It's a sign!" I think she will eventually have great success introducing her Active Modern clothing line right here in town. But, for the present, "I'll start small," she says.

Now, I need to find employment for myself. I know I am definitely happier since we've arrived in Banff. That I do know. But I feel my life would be so much better if I were doing something productive. It's odd how teaching prospects don't appeal to me at the moment. I'm surprised. There's an impressive brick and stone schoolhouse here so perhaps I'll apply for a position if nothing else presents itself. Right now, I think I'm looking for a new opportunity. When I mention these recent thoughts to my mother, she just shakes her head and can only say, "Well . . . I never."

Journal Entry

July 30, 1916

I suppose we appear odd to these townsfolk, two women without husbands, on our own. We think sometimes we should make up a suitable story to explain why we aren't married. I see the admiration for us in the eyes of the people as we walk about. I know we could easily have suitors despite the lack of men. For now, I follow Mama's lead in this regard. We seem to provide each other with the relationship we find most rewarding. Often, we talk about how it appears to others that we have put our own needs first over having husbands and children. All good and well for Mama; she has her child. Maybe someday I'll have the same. My thoughts about personal choices are becoming tangled again. For now, I leave the gossipers to their gossip.

The hotel owners, Louise and Robert Townsend, have even given us a cut-rate on our rooms because they can see we're planning to put down roots here in Banff. It feels so good to think we might have found a new community.

******

"Mama, I've just had the best day!"

Her mother is sitting by the window placing delicate stitches into the hem of a garment.

"Always good to hear. Tell me what's happened," Mary responds, putting aside her piecework.

"Well, I noticed several large wooden boxes being unloaded off the back of a truck, just down the street. Several men were carting these heavy boxes into a building, which is going to be . . . the new Banff Mountain Weekly! Mama, it's going to be a newspaper office! And I think, after meeting the owners, Edward, and Emily Taylor . . . that I might approach them for work! I could soon be writing for a newspaper! Also, we are meeting tomorrow morning to discuss what I could possibly contribute. I told them I have absolutely NO newspaper experience but I'm an avid writer and reader . . . and already I have some ideas!"

Journal Entry

August 10, 1916

I presented (what I considered) my three best pieces of writing to Edward and Emily. When they put my samples aside (to be read later, they said), I confess it was not what I expected. They do, however, seem like lovely people, and I think it would be a joy to work with them.

It appears they are looking for someone to take care of all their advertising. The job requires approaching Banff's business community plus regular townsfolk who wish to rent space in the newspaper. This is not quite what I had anticipated but still, it's a way to meet absolutely everyone in town. I think I would be good at talking people into the benefits of business promotion. This little weekly newspaper is exactly what Banff needs. Edward and Emily seem to think I'd be the perfect "emissary for this mission" and recounted their first reactions when I bounced into their new offices looking for work. They both perform (I must admit) hilarious impressions of my overly exuberant nature.

Journal Entry

September 1, 1917

My thoughts today are back in my little prairie schoolhouse. A new teacher is getting ready to enrol all those sweet familiar faces.

Pyotr's little freckle-faced Eva will now be entering Grade 4. One of the fathers will have brought in a load of firewood for the schoolroom stove. Another parent will have brought in a few hay bales for the stables. In my mind I can see the children walking along the country roads, books in hand, kicking rocks as they make their way to school. The few who still ride their horses will be entering the barn and unsaddling. Fall harvest crews will be starting to assemble. These melancholy moments come and go.

Journal Entry

October 12, 1917

The Taylor's are very pleased with my efforts in gaining advertising clientele. I'm a bit surprised how persuasive I can be, but not Mama. "Always knew you could talk the hind leg off a mule," she says to me. There are two general stores and a pharmacy on the main street that have even promised monthly renewals. Robert Carson's cooperage wants ad space in the next five *issues! The owners of Ho Fat's Chinese Restaurant also want a regular monthly ad space even though there are only four tables available. Also, they will soon be moving their laundry business to a new location and want advertisements for the grand opening. Their Chinese Market Garden is also doing a booming business and they're eager to rent additional newspaper space for that as well. When I approached the Banff Hotel as a possible client, I was told by the concierge that all their advertising was handled by the CPR railroad, and they had no need for my services. However, after a little persistence, I was directed to speak with the hotel's Chief Tourism Officer who was only too happy to listen to some of my suggestions. It seems there are hot pools near the hotel (Mama and I <u>definitely</u> need to actively investigate this curiosity immediately!) and he would like more publicity for this as a tourist draw. So, now it seems I have another job. I'm writing an advertisement for travellers to be placed on the trains when they pull into the station. Life is just full of surprises.*

Journal Entry

September 10, 1918

After being in charge of advertisements for the last year, I have finally been moved to our newly created "SPECIAL FEATURES" section! The Taylor's newspaper has expanded just like the town. Edward and Emily have given me a great chance to fine-tune my writing skills and I must not squander this opportunity on frivolous reporting.

Mama and I were treated to a great celebratory dinner at the Ho Fat by the Townsends from the hotel and their two children. We were also joined by the Taylors. Mr. and Mrs. Stubbs from the Grain and Feed General Store arrived later with their children, so Ho Fat and I moved all the restaurant tables together. We had such great fun, and the party went on until all the children grew tired and cranky. Even Mama had to leave early because she was tuckered out.

Journal Entry

November 11, 1918

*I was in the middle of writing a piece about the railway forcing the Indigenous Stoney Nation people off their land when suddenly, Marion Simmonds from the post office rushed through our front doors with the most exciting news **of this century!** A truce has been declared in Europe! The Great War is over! We all gathered on the streets and went completely mad!*

Journal Entry

January 1, 1919

This must have been the best Christmas and New Year's celebrations ever. The school choirs circulated through town on Christmas Eve singing carols and then the whole town gathered in the municipal hall for mulled wine (shocking!) and shortbread. The Banff Hotel hosted a New Year's Eve dance in its very elegant ballroom followed by a potluck dinner after midnight. Such a happy New Year.

My mother is still feeling poorly, which is quite unlike her, but she did leave her bed to hear the choirs. I know she was sorry to miss the big hotel shindig. Her seamstress work is also abandoned for now (which she hates) but it's evident how tired she is. She is unhappy feeling so fatigued and finds it difficult to breathe. Despite her objections, I'm taking her to see the doctor tomorrow! I'll also have a checkup. All these celebrations and late nights are also beginning to take a toll on me.

Journal Entry

January 3, 1919

An odd memory tugs at me. I am thinking of a severe snowstorm one winter. After the devastation passed and the brightest blue skies returned, Mama and I started to dig ourselves out from the mountains of deep snow. We spent a whole morning clearing the pathways between our little house, the school, and the barn. Suddenly, looking up, we see Pyotr and his grandmother arriving by horse drawn sleigh. He proudly announced, "sour borscht soup and rye bread! For you!" I can still see his horses. They are gingerly stepping through the drifts, kicking up glistening sprays of frothy white foam. Gallant noble knight.

Journal Entry

January 5, 1919

My "FEATURES" piece this week is titled, "THE CHRISTMAS ARMISTICE OF 1914," a wartime remembrance article. I think about all those Allied and German soldiers during their ceasefire, mutually celebrating December 25. As the bullets and bombs gradually stopped, they slowly emerged from their muddy trenches and crossed no man's land to meet their enemy in the middle. How strange for them, knowing that the very men they were bartering with for cigarettes or playing football with would be the same soldiers they would shoot at when the fighting resumed the next day.

At the end of this Great War, I share in the overwhelming relief of escape from the bad news we have come to expect over the past four years. Until all this uncertainty ended, did we realize how we collectively held our breath? Notifications of our fallen soldiers have caused far too many mothers and children unfathomable grief. Unfortunately, the ravages of the Spanish Influenza now follows cruelly on the astounding loss of thousands of our military.

Journal Entry

January 15, 1919

I have returned from visiting Mama in her assigned hospital ward. The nurses finally allowed me only the briefest of masked visitations because of rampant infection risks. No curtains divided her from her neighbours in the next beds. Our grief was open for all to see. They tell me she is near the end. Her eyes were closed. She didn't know I was there. I can't bear it. Her sweet wee ashen face. This woman once convinced me as a child that she knew a secret bird language.

******

The loss of my own life and that of my wonderful mother has rendered us a sad part of Canada's death statistics from the deadly Spanish Influenza.

Today, Mama and I returned in spirit from the mountains of Banff to our first prairie home. We are on our familiar dirt road, bordered by the wide expanses of wheat, leading to my little country schoolhouse. We see a few students playing outside. Since it's harvest time, perhaps the majority of the children are helping out at home or in the fields bringing in the harvest. We visit the townsite and see it's also quite deserted. It's noon and the sun is beating down intensely, forcing people into the shade. I would like to visit Pyotr's homestead but first we will follow the road out of town, past the derelict Three Sisters, those scandalous old houses of ill repute.

Then we will make our way toward the river.

CHAPTER 14

EVA

We are watching a woman standing at the edge of a massive field of flowering rape seed. Even in the fading light, she squints at its shocking shade of mustard yellow. In a movie, this is where the violins would swell. Picture a blazing orange and pink sky behind a lowering sun. The silhouettes of trees are turning black. The year is 1938 and this woman has just returned to her father's Saskatchewan homestead for a deathbed visit.

Pyotr is lying in the rough-hewn bed he built, in the main bedroom of the log house he also built, on the quarter section of his original homestead. She leans over the bed to kiss him good night.

Pyotr's vocal ramblings are endless and repetitive. He lies amongst the damp and rumpled sheets. He slips in and out of his own sense of time, occasionally recognizing her for who she is, or sometimes calling her by the names of her two younger sisters.

This is Eva, eldest daughter of Pyotr, granddaughter of Sonia, his beloved Babushka. Sometimes she is Natalia, Eva's mother, but more often she is . . . Lizzie? How is it, Eva thinks that he would conjure the name of her favourite childhood teacher?

"You sit your horse well," he says aloud to his assembled bedside mourners.

"You're a good teacher, Pyotr," is the response from his imagined companion.

He repeats these exact words out loud, as he has done in his memory for decades. Eva and her two sisters have heard this one-sided conversation before. They glance at each other, avoiding their mother's eyes. They secretly know where he is in his recollections and who he is talking to.

When Pyotr was about twenty, a meeting was arranged by his community elders. It was a meeting for him to meet a possible future wife, Natalia. Natalia lived in Edenbridge, which was an Eastern Saskatchewan Jewish settlement about eighty miles from Pyotr's homestead. Their arranged meeting was tense and awkward, but Pyotr was instantly struck by her fair hair and freckled beauty. Natalia reminded him strongly of his first love and he found himself easily transposing Natalia's face for . . . Lizzie's.

"He has always been so physically strong," sighs Natalia as she sits by Pyotr's bedside. "How could his body still be so strong . . . and his mind so poor . . . just look at his hands . . . have you ever seen such a hand?"

It was true. Eva now sits on the bed beside her mother and picks up one of Pyotr's large hands. She turns it over to rub her thumbs on that familiar hardened layer of smoothened calluses. It has always reminded her of the feel of solid saddle leather. She remembers when her father would hoist her high up onto his shoulders with those strong hands. His treasured cat Myushka, angry at being displaced, would sit on the ground with her back toward them while Pyotr and Eva would gallop around the yard playing horsey. Eva could remember her mother and Pyotr's grandmother watching them and laughing. He would always tease them, saying, "I'm surrounded by the constant demands of so many women! Only females in my life! How to keep all of you happy? You wear me out! There is nothing left. I'm empty!"

If Pyotr ever felt sorry for lacking a son, he never made his three girls question the value of their gender. It was always his wife Natalia who would look longingly at the small boys of her women friends and sadly shrug, "I only know how to make girls. What can I say?"

Was a boy necessary for a successful farm? Pyotr, with the assistance of his wife and indomitable grandmother had created a remarkably prosperous quarter section of land that had withstood the challenges of establishing his homesteading title, rejected the allure of enlistment in Britain's Great War of 1914, evaded the devastating Spanish Influenza which followed, and finally endured the Depression. Pyotr had successfully acquitted himself by understanding the need for improved farming techniques like contour terracing and crop rotation. His land had luckily escaped most of the topsoil loss experienced by the homesteaders of the Southern Palliser. Canada's Prairie Rehabilitation Programme had also provided financial assistance during Saskatchewan's prolonged drought.

To be a farmer was by no means an easy task, he would repeatedly tell Eva. This would be followed by his favourite joke, "and, what do you call a farmer? He is a man outstanding in his field." They would repeat this punchline together and happily chuckle with each other. She took comfort in knowing that's how her father always saw himself. A simple, uncomplicated man who, when shirtless, displayed the telltale signs of a farmer's tan.

"Come with me. I have a surprise for you," he murmurs aloud in his delirium.

In his mind, Pyotr sees himself leading Lizzie through a grove of trees to a clearing where his grandmother stands with her back to them, stripping 12 foot lengths of cut willow poles. The discarded bark and leaves lie at her feet.

"This will be my new log house in about a year and I would like to share it with you," he says to Lizzie.

"With . . . me? Pyotr, what are you saying? I'm not sure I understand."

"I want the two of us to live here with Baba. And your mother, of course. Lizzie, I am loving you. I have said this to you so many times and I hope you love me."

He sees Lizzie now as she turns her disbelieving face toward him and stammers how she needs time to think about what he is saying.

"Are you proposing to me?" he hears her ask. "Are you asking me to marry you?"

And now it is Pyotr who is at a loss for words. He feels disheartened by her lack of a positive response. He watches as the two of them return to their horses and without speaking, make their way back to Lizzie's schoolhouse.

******

He would proudly take his daughters with him whenever he left the farm, Eva remembers. We were by his side during town hall meetings, barn raisings, cattle auctions, and community dances. She could recollect, more than once, glancing over at her wonderful father, sitting in profile, elbows on knees, studiously assessing the merits of whatever livestock he wanted to purchase. He always looked like he was facing a harsh prairie wind with his eyes kind of squinty and intense. But then, he'd turn and see her face and break out into a wide grin.

One day, when she was in high school, her father suggested that she leave the farm after school finished that year and enter into training to be a nurse in the capital city. The qualifications in those days were only the completion of Grade 11 and an interest in medical assistance. She was beside herself with excitement and the prospects of living in a big city was overwhelming. Her mother was dumbfounded and quite angry with Pyotr's idea. Natalia felt Eva was too young to be unsupervised and off on her own. She would be living in residence without parental supervision. Natalia was also quite jealous that Pyotr continually singled Eva out for special consideration. Eva knew he had always favoured her. Her younger sisters were more like their mother: quiet and lacking curiosity. But they were happy for Eva and with their blessing, she was only too thrilled to get a chance to see the world. While Regina wasn't exactly the world, it was a start.

******

"But I know you **love** your teaching. If you became my wife, would you have to leave it?"

These mumbled words circled the heads of those surrounding his reclining body. But even then Pyotr knew if working women became wives, they were forced back into the home.

At moments like this, Natalia would gaze off into the distance, unsure of how to explain her husband's rambling words to herself let alone her children. She has always known in her heart that he had loved another before her. She saw it repeatedly when he would stumble over her name or call out in their shared moments of ecstasy. But she knew, in his own way, Pyotr loved her. She understood their union was something he respected.

******

During her first two years in the nurses' residence, Eva returned home as often as she was able. With every visit her family remarked on her changing appearance. Her new short, finger-waved hair created more conversation than she felt was necessary. It was only her father who showed any interest in her nursing studies. Eva's mother and sisters rarely asked any questions about her classes or her new friends, instead focusing on the romantic possibilities for Eva's younger sisters. When Eva was assigned fieldwork in her third year of training, she was placed at the same hospital where she had lived in residence. Pyotr gave her the money she needed to buy a used car so her visits home could become more frequent.

On one of those visits, the two of them rode out on horseback to the buffalo pound Pyotr loved to visit. On that bright spring afternoon, he was showing intermittent signs of the mental decline that Eva had come to recognize.

"You love this place for its history, don't you?" Eva asked her father.

"I think I love it because you have always loved it so much."

Eva knew, as he said this that he was talking to someone else.

"You would tell me how you would try to recreate the drama for your students. You would tell me how you could actually see them herding the frenzied buffalo toward the cliff edge. You would say how you could hear the warriors whooping while they chased and directed the snorting stampede. You would tell me how you could imagine them readying their arrows. You would tell me how you could visualize the herd running to the cliff and then falling to their deaths on the hard ground below."

"Poppa, it's Eva here with you now . . . I think you are talking to someone else."

But he was gone again, into his own head and could not answer.

One evening as Natalia and her daughters are sitting by Pyotr's bed, he suddenly opened his eyes and started to sit up.

"What a complete surprise to see you," he said, "and . . . you've brought your mother. I am so glad to see you both."

As he stared toward the empty doorway, the remainder of what he says becomes lost in mumbled fragments. It is a conversation that only he can hear. Eva and her sisters glance at each other, knowing with certainty that he thinks of another.

******

She misses having her father in the audience during her graduation ceremonies. Eva's mother and sisters sit quite close, in the front row, and beam with pride. Eva's future nursing plans were already in place even before this graduation event was scheduled.

What Eva doesn't know when she accepted her position in a British hospital for convalescing veterans is that in the following year, 1939, Canada will again be involved in another great European war. And when she eventually meets young Flight Captain Henry Goodfellow (nicknamed Small), of the Saskatchewan Air Command Unit 75, whose unconscious body was rescued when his plane was shot down over the English Channel, the two of them will find they have much which connects them.

EPILOGUE

From 1910 onward, anyone travelling through a certain area of south central Saskatchewan could not fail to notice the three old houses standing alone on the open prairie. For four decades they remained deserted, outside of Saskatoon's city limits and served as very useful landmarks.

Today, another young girl on her bicycle is seen leaning on the handlebars of her bike while watching a bulldozer demolish one of those old houses. It's 1953 and a new firehall will soon be erected where this *Sister* stood. The other two houses will remain in place and become part of Saskatchewan's pioneer heritage. They are currently located on a residential street in Saskatoon.

Author's Note

Several writings inspired this novella:

1. A History of Saskatchewan's Early Sex Trade, Lisa Buchanan, Oct. 8, 2012.
   (This was part of The Young Innovators Series, 2012, The Saskatoon Star Phoenix.)
2. The Last Spike, Pierre Burton, 1971.
3. The Promised Land, Pierre Burton, 1984.
4. Vimy, Pierre Burton, 1986.
5. Child Labor and the Industrial Revolution, Harriet Isecke, 2009.
6. Tales from the Homestead: A History of Prairie Pioneers 1867–1914, Sandra Rollings-Magnusson, 2022.

www.ingramcontent.com/pod-product-compliance
Lightning Source LLC
LaVergne TN
LVHW041636060526
838200LV00040B/1597